lonely planet

POCKET

LAS VEGAS

TOP EXPERIENCES • LOCAL LIFE

T0022735

**ANDREA SCHULTE-PEEVERS,
BENEDICT WALKER**

Las Vegas

Plan Your Trip

Neon Museum (p125)
MARK READ/LONELY PLANET ©

COVID-19

We have re-checked every business in this book before publication to ensure that it is still open after the COVID-19 outbreak. However, the economic and social impacts of COVID-19 will continue to be felt long after the outbreak has been contained, and many businesses, services and events referenced in this guide may experience ongoing restrictions. Some may be temporarily closed, have changed their opening hours and services, or require bookings; some unfortunately could have closed permanently. We suggest you check with venues before visiting for the latest information.

Welcome to Las Vegas

Vegas, baby! An oasis of indulgence dazzling in the desert. The Strip shimmers hypnotically, promising excitement, entertainment, fortune and fame. Where else can you spend the night partying in ancient Rome, wake up for brunch beneath the Eiffel Tower, watch an erupting volcano at sunset and get married in a pink Cadillac? All in Sin City. It's yours for the taking.

Welcome to Las Vegas Sign

Top Experiences

TUPUNGATO/SHUTTERSTOCK ©

Enjoy the Opulence at Bellagio (p38)

KIT LEONG/SHUTTERSTOCK ©

Soak up the City's Colorful Mob History (p116)

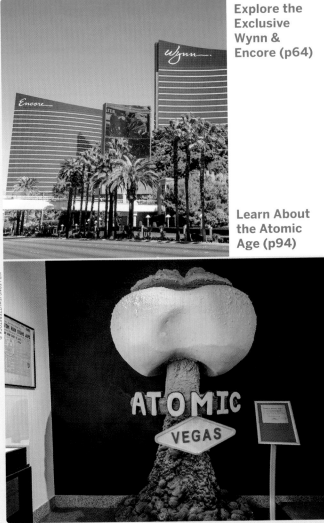

Explore the Exclusive Wynn & Encore (p64)

Learn About the Atomic Age (p94)

Plan Your Trip Top Experiences

KOBBY DAGAN/SHUTTERSTOCK ©

KIT LEONG/SHUTTERSTOCK ©

Be Dazzled by Glittering Mandalay Bay (p42)

USA-PYON/SHUTTERSTOCK ©

ALIZADA STUDIOS/SHUTTERSTOCK ©

Explore New York in Miniature (p46)

Strike Gold at a Classy Old-School Casino (p114)

TRAVELVIEW/SHUTTERSTOCK ©

ROI061/SHUTTERSTOCK ©

Wander the LINQ Promenade (p50)

Admire Art and Architecture at CityCenter (p52)

Climb the Eiffel Tower (p56)

Ride a Gondola at Venetian & Palazzo (p60)

Visit an Oasis in the Desert (p104)

Dining Out

The Strip has been studded with celebrity chefs for years. All-you-can-eat buffets and $10 steaks still exist, but today's high-rolling visitors demand ever more sophisticated dining experiences, with meals designed – although not personally prepared – by famous taste-makers.

Celebs in the Kitchen

After Wolfgang Puck brought Spago to Caesars Palace in 1992, celebrity chefs opened branches at every megaresort, including Bobby Flay, Mario Batali, and Nobu Matsuhisa. Note that most have nothing to do with the day-to-day running of their namesake Vegas kitchens.

Scoring a Table

Most restaurants take reservations for dinner and sometimes lunch. Call ahead or book online through the restaurant, the free OpenTable website (www.opentable.com) and mobile app, or ask your hotel concierge for help, but be prepared to tip $10 to reserve the best tables.

Local Eats

Venture Downtown or east and west of the Strip for local drinking and dining for far less than restaurants on the Strip. Not only will you get better gastronomic bang for your buck, you'll be able to take a little bite of everything from authentic Thai street snacks and Neapolitan pizzas to Asian-Mexican fusion tacos and crazy food-truck creations.

Celebrity Chefs

Restaurant Guy Savoy This is the only US restaurant by three-star Michelin chef Guy Savoy. (p79)

Joël Robuchon 'Chef of the century' Robuchon's eponymous restaurant lives up to the hype. (p78)

Border Grill Weekend brunches are best at this TV-celeb modern Mexican joint. (p79)

Guy Fieri's Vegas Kitchen & Bar *Diners, Drive-ins and Dives* everyday hero's foray onto the Vegas food scene. (p76)

RITU MANOJ JETHANI/SHUTTERSTOCK ©

Table with a View

Top of the World You'll pay for the incredible views from Vegas' highest revolving restaurant. (p80)

Todd English's Olives You can't get closer to the Fountains of Bellagio than at this smart eatery. (p82)

Twist by Pierre Gagnaire Enjoy romantic views from this Michelin-hatted French restaurant. (p55)

Eiffel Tower Restaurant Perched high on the Eiffel Tower, above the Fountains of Bellagio. Say no more. (p57)

Rivea Delano's rooftop sensation has spectacular views from the southern Strip. (p80)

Japanese Cuisine

Raku Authenticity without celebrity reigns at this off-Strip sushi joint and *robata* grill. (p105)

Morimoto It's hard to resist TV's Iron Chef Masaharu Morimoto's inventive fusion of Japanese and American cuisine. (p78)

Nobu Iron Chef 'Nobu' Matsuhisa's sequel to his trendsetting NYC establishment. (p81)

Steakhouses

Bazaar Meat Next-gen steakhouse with global influences. (p79)

Stripsteak A stylishly minimalist steakhouse with all-natural beef and unusual gourmet sides. (p81)

SW Steakhouse Classic cuts by the side of a pint-sized lake. (p67)

Vegas Buffets 🍽️

Many of Vegas' famous all-you-can-eat buffets closed when COVID-19 hit, but they're coming back: **Wicked Spoon** (p82), **Buffet at Wynn** (p80), **Bacchanal** (p80; pictured), **Buffet at Bellagio** (p82) are some favorites. Show up early to avoid long lines.

Treasure Hunt

Surprisingly, Vegas has evolved into a sophisticated shopping destination. Purveyors of haute couture on the Strip cater to a cashed-up clientele, whether it's catwalk fashions, diamond jewels once worn by royalty or sports cars. But Sin City is still the kind of place where porn-star-worthy bling, Elvis wigs and other tacky souvenirs fly off the shelves.

What to Buy

If all you want is a T-shirt or shot glass inscribed with 'Fabulous Las Vegas,' cheap souvenirs are everywhere. But if you're looking for something more unusual, the city's specialty shops are full of cool kitsch and collectibles, from vintage casino memorabilia to showgirls' feather boas.

Glamour Shopping

The Strip's shopping action is dominated by megamalls such as the Fashion Show and the Grand Canal Shoppes at the Venetian and Palazzo. Upscale boutiques await inside CityCenter's airy Crystals mall and luxe casino resorts like Wynn & Encore, Palazzo and Bellagio. Meanwhile, the hip Cosmopolitan casino resort collects the Strip's most eclectic indie and designer shops.

Off-Strip Finds

Downtown you'll find tacky souvenirs, but also cool vintage-clothing stores, antiques shops and art galleries, especially on Fremont St east of Las Vegas Blvd and in the 18b Arts District. Head west of the Strip to stock up on adult toys, trashy lingerie, 'exotic' dance wear and go-go boots. East of the Strip near University of Nevadad Las Vegas, Maryland Pkwy is chock-a-block with cheapo shops.

Fashion

Fashion Show 'The Cloud,' a futuristic-looking steel canopy, tops off this giant and flashy mall that hosts live catwalk shows. (p88)

Grand Canal Shoppes at the Palazzo Anchored by the three-story department store Barneys New York, the Palazzo's shops are dazzling. (p63)

Grand Canal Shoppes at the Venetian This airy Italianate mall adorned

DCSTOCKPHOTOGRAPHY/SHUTTERSTOCK ©

with frescoes has over 80 luxury boutiques. (p63)

Shops at Cosmopolitan Hipster-loving boutiques gather inside the Cosmopolitan resort. (p89)

Shopping Malls

Shops at Crystals The most striking shopping center on the Strip for those with cash to burn. (p88)

Miracle Mile Shops A 1.2-mile-long mall with over 170 retailers and some of the best department stores in the US. (p89)

The Forum Shops at Caesars Trendy labels in a swish Roman marketplace anchored by a giant aquarium and a hilarious animatronic show. (p89)

Only in Vegas

Gamblers General Store Nevada's largest inventory of vintage and new slot machines! (p131)

Rainbow Feather Dyeing Co A fabulous selection of feathers and fans for showgirls, in every possible hue. (p131)

Bonanza Gift Shop It's a blast wading through this enormous, tacky selection of souvenirs. (p91)

Houdini's Magic Shop Get your magician memorabilia and DIY magic kits here. (p91)

Worth a Trip

Oozing sophistication, **Downtown Summerlin** (☎702-832-1000; www.downtown summerlin.com; 1980 Festival Plaza Dr; ⏰10am-9pm Mon-Sat, 11am-7pm Sun; 🛜🚻👶; 🚌206, SX) is one of Las Vegas' most attractive outdoor shopping, dining and recreational complexes, filled with fancy boutiques and bigger department stores like Macy's and Dillard's. On Saturdays, it hosts a fantastic farmers market.

Bar Open

It's no secret that Las Vegas is party central – the Strip is ground zero for some of the country's hottest clubs and most happening bars, where you never know who you'll be rubbing shoulders with. But what you might not know is that Downtown's Fremont East Entertainment District is the go-to place for Vegas' coolest nonmainstream haunts.

Hitting the Clubs

No expense has been spared to bring nightclubs in the Strip's megaresorts on a par with Los Angeles and New York City. Wildly extravagant dancefloors are like a Hollywood set designer's dream. Many clubs tend to play it safe, spinning mainstream grooves and mash-ups, but top-tier nightspots also jet in famous DJs from North America, Europe and beyond. In summer, daytime pool clubs are all the rage. Expect killer DJs, bikini-clad cocktail servers and a less-is-more dress code.

Getting Past the Velvet Rope

Typical cover charges at nightclubs are $50 on weekends and $20 on weeknights, with women usually paying less. VIP and front-of-the-line passes are sold on websites such as www.vegas.com. Also check the club's website for guest list spots or make VIP bottle-service reservations.

Raising the Bar

Many bars stay open until the wee hours, and some never close. There's also an extremely liberal policy when it comes to drinking in public, especially on the Strip and at Downtown's Fremont Street Experience.

Cocktail Bars

Skyfall Lounge Sit and sip cocktails and gaze upon spectacular sunsets over the Spring Mountains. (p43; pictured)

Parasol Up & Parasol Down It doesn't get much more stylish than this plush, two-level cocktail bar, at Wynn. (p67)

KIT LEONG/SHUTTERSTOCK ©

Chandelier Lounge Shimmering strands of glass beads connect three floors of cocktail wizardry at this ab-fab lounge. (p85)

Downtown Cocktail Room Classic cocktails and modern twists make this low-lit speakeasy undeniably romantic. (p130)

Nightclubs

Drai's Beachclub & Nightclub Legendary after-hours parties are known for an outrageous bottle list and celebrity drop-ins. (p85)

Hakkasan Unstoppable resident DJs Tiësto and Steve Aoki rule the roost of VIP booths and floor-to-ceiling LEDs. (p82)

XS Heavyweight decksmiths rule the dancefloor while high rollers pose at private poolside cabanas. (p84).

Jewel The successor to Aria's Haze offers a more intimate alternative to the megaclubs. (p84)

Rooftop Bars

Commonwealth Too cool for school? No way! Plush booths, softly lit chandeliers and a killer rooftop patio. (p119)

Beer Park Beneath the Eiffel Tower, overlooking the Fountains of Bellagio and countless beers on tap. (p57)

Skyfall Lounge Unparalleled views of the southern Strip from atop Mandalay Bay's Delano hotel. (p43)

Pool Bars

Mandalay Bay Beach Eleven acres of beach, 2700 tons of Californian sand and up to 6ft waves. Gnarly! (p43)

Wet Republic Think of MGM Grand's 'ultra pool' as a nightclub brought into the light of day. (p84)

Encore Beach Club It doesn't get more exotic or exclusive than this decadent beach club. (p85)

Marquee From late spring through early fall, Cosmo's megapopular daytime pool club rocks the rooftop above the Strip. (p83)

Casinos

You're on your third martini. You just won the last three hands. Adrenaline pumping, you double down – and lose the down payment on your next car. Gambling is no question part of the Vegas experience. Have fun, but understand the games you're playing and stop when you're ahead.

The House Always Wins

For every game except poker, the house has a statistical winning edge over the gambler and for nearly every payout, it 'holds' a small portion of the winnings. Amounts vary with the game and with individual bets, but in the long run, you're ensured to lose everything that you gamble.

Know When to Hold 'Em

Traditional casino games include poker, baccarat, craps, roulette and slot machines. You must be at least 21 to play or even hang around in a casino. Every game has its own customs, traditions and strategies. Almost all casinos hand out guides on the game and may offer free one-hour lessons by pros; these include Texas Hold'em, blackjack and dice rollin' craps.

Slot Action

Slots are wildly popular and pretty simple – you just put money in and pull the handle (or push a button). The probabilities are programmed into the machine, and the chances of winning (or losing) are the same on every pull. Careful: in Sin City, these money-gobbling machines are nicknamed 'one-armed bandits' for a reason...

High Rollers

Wynn & Encore Casinos The sassy Wynn and Encore sisters boast in excess of 1900 gaming machines and 160 tables. (p64)

Palazzo The younger sibling and extension of the Venetian is a true high-roller's casino. Together they form Vegas' largest gaming floor. (p60)

Cosmopolitan The only gaming area in Vegas with floor-to-ceiling windows overlooking the Strip. (p53)

Aria This sleek casino floor has an overwhelming 2000 slot machines. (p53)

Bellagio This luxurious casino with its famous fountain

TUPUNGATO/SHUTTERSTOCK ©

show featured in the 2001 *Ocean's Eleven*. (p38)

Mandalay Bay Poolside slots and a luxe, resort-style feel set Mandalay Bay apart. (p42)

Casinos for Sightseeing

Golden Nugget Home of the 'Hand of Faith,' the heftiest hunk of gold ever dug up. (p114)

Caesars Palace The Roman Empire–inspired resort served as the setting for *The Hangover*. (p73; pictured)

Circus Circus An enormous clown-shaped marquee and tent-shaped casino under a gaudily striped big top.

Luxor Your chance to gamble inside a faux Egyptian pyramid. (p75)

Old-School Gambling

El Cortez A smoky, retro classic with a grassroots crowd. (p127)

Main Street Station Gamble among the antiques and beneath art nouveau chandeliers. (p127)

Golden Gate A gambling hall has stood on this spot since 1906. (p126)

Locals' Favorites

Palms Fans of MTV's *Real World: Las Vegas* will recognize this hypermodern den that claims 'looser' slots than most. (p108)

Gold Coast Old-fashioned gambling lair beloved for its low-roller roulette and traditional Chinese dim sum and dumplings. (p108)

Top Tips

○ If you're a novice, get your feet wet with low-stakes craps.

○ Drinks are free when you're playing, but don't forget to tip the server at least $1 per drink.

○ The cheapest table games – and highest concentration of local gamblers – are Downtown.

Show Time

That sensory overload of blindingly bright neon lights means you've finally landed on Las Vegas Blvd. The infamous Strip has the lion's share of gigantic casino hotels, all flashily competing to lure you (and your wallet) inside, with larger-than-life production shows, celebrity-filled nightclubs and burlesque cabarets. Head off-Strip to find jukebox dive bars, arty cocktail lounges, strip clubs and more.

What's On

The whirling Cirque du Soleil empire keeps expanding with such recent additions as *Beatles LOVE* and *Michael Jackson ONE* as well as the fantastical variety show *Zarkana*. Old-school shows at smaller casinos feature hokey song, dance and magic numbers that often don't follow a story line. Sin City's new breed of bawdy, hilarious variety shows are staged cabaret-style in unusual venues, mostly on the Strip.

Getting Tickets

Most Vegas ticket outlets apply a commission for each ticket sold. All but the biggest-ticket shows are up for grabs in-person only at **Tix 4 Tonight** (www.tix4tonight.com), a chain of same-day, discount ticket outlets. Get in line before 10am for the best selection. The website has a list of locations. Alternatively, try **Vegas.com**, which sells tickets to high-profile and low-budget shows, special events and touring exhibitions, plus nightclub VIP and front-of-the-line passes. Of course, there's always **Ticketmaster** (www.ticketsmaster.com), a broker for megaconcerts and sporting events.

Spectacles & Shows

Le Rêve the Dream Cirque du Soleil's surreal Dream plays out underwater in a custom-built pool. (p65)

O A spectacular feat of engineering, this original aquatic masterpiece explores the history of theater. (p41)

Beatles LOVE Beatlemania is back! All your favorite tunes fused with dance and aerial acrobatics. (p86; pictured)

Michael Jackson ONE Showstopping dancers and lithe acrobats bring MJ's greatest hits to life. (p45)

DIEGO GRANDI/ALAMY STOCK PHOTO ©

Blue Man Group Art, music, technology and comedy combine in one of Vegas' most popular, family-friendly shows. (p86)

Free Entertainment

Circus Circus This cheesy casino has free circus acts and loads of family fun. (74)

Fountains of Bellagio A visit to Vegas is incomplete without snapping these free dancing fountains. (p39)

Mirage Volcano As gaudy as it gets, this may be the closest you'll come to a volcanic eruption. (p75)

Fremont Street Experience A five-block pedestrian mall, illuminated at night and chock-full of entertainment. (p128)

Comedy & Magic

Penn & Teller This intellectual odd couple have struck the balance between magic and comedy. (p111)

Criss Angel Mindfreak Live Billed as the greatest magic spectacle of all time. (p87)

Carrot Top Find out why this wild, orange-haired comedian has audiences begging for more. (p87)

Music Venues

House of Blues This cool, Southern-style venue features live soul, pop, rock, country, jazz and, of course, blues. (p45)

Brooklyn Bowl Hip NYC import does triple duty as bowling alley, restaurant and concert venue for indie bands. (p51)

Le Cabaret Free live jazz and sultry lounge music in an intimate venue at Paris Las Vegas. (p59)

Major Venues

Colosseum There's hardly a bad seat in the house at Caesars Palace's 4100-seat theater-in-the-round. (p87)

Smith Center for the Performing Arts An architecturally beautiful multivenue complex in Downtown's Symphony Park. (p131)

Park Theater Opening in 2016, this sexy, avant-garde theater pulls in A-list artists. (p87)

T-Mobile Arena In the heart of the Strip, this state-of-the-art arena, new in 2016, seats up to 20,000. (p87)

Local Culture

It's easy to forget that there's a city beyond the Strip – and a fascinating one at that. There's the hipster scene Downtown, where you can rub shoulders with locals at indie music venues. Nearby, vintage neon signs hark back to Vegas' early days, while west of the Strip, the impressive Springs Preserve connects you with local natural history.

A Growing Arts Scene

Arts and culture in Las Vegas would, until recently, have been just another oxymoron. That's no longer the case, with a thriving Downtown arts scene, a couple of Smithsonian-affiliated museums and UNLV's Performing Arts Center all being rewarding cultural destinations.

Passion for the Game

You can wager on just about anything at race and sports books inside casinos, and nearly every watering hole runs Monday Night Football specials. World-class championship boxing draws fans from all over the globe, and weekend 'fight nights' are huge on the Strip.

Head for the Hills

Options suitable for easy day trips include Red Rock Canyon National Conservation Area, which has hiking and rock climbing. There's good mountain biking outside Boulder City, while Lake Mead beckons with boating, fishing and other water sports.

Drinking & Partying

Double Down Saloon Mix with the lunatic fringe at this dark, psychedelic gin joint that never closes. (p100)

Commonwealth Raise your pinkie with old-fashioned cocktails on the rooftop patio or in the plush Prohibition-style interior. (p119)

Firefly Mingle with fashionable local folk over tapas and late-night drinks on the patio. (p98)

First Friday Community-arts-festival-cum-street-party in Downtown's Arts District on the first Friday of the month. (p130)

KIT LEONG/SHUTTERSTOCK ©

History

National Atomic Testing Museum Delve into Sin City's dark atomic past, when people came out for the mushroom clouds. (p94)

Pinball Hall of Fame Retro fun in a wonderland of vintage pinball machines and video games. (p98)

Welcome to Las Vegas Sign Arrive after dark for maximum 'wows' when cruising past this iconic 1950s neon sign. (p74)

Springs Preserve This educational complex is a rewarding trip through historical, cultural and biological time. (p104)

Nevada State Museum Mammoths to mobsters, Hoover Dam to atomic bombs, this museum's got Sin City's milestones covered. (p105)

Watching Sports

Triple 7 Lively Monday Night Football on the screens and great microbrews on tap. (p130; pictured)

Caesars Palace One of many popular sports books in town, this casino offers special menus and customized 'man caves' for major sporting events. (p73)

Mandalay Bay Events Center High-profile boxing matches, plus ultimate fighting. (p45)

Worth a Trip

Las Vegas Premium Outlets North (📞702-474-7500; www.premiumoutlets.com/vegasnorth; 875 S Grand Central Pkwy; 🕐11am-7pm Mon-Sat, noon-6pm Sun; 📶♿; 🚌207) Brand-name bargain hunters head to Vegas' jam-packed outlet malls. The best of the bunch is this retail haven with designer names including Armani, DKNY, Dolce & Gabbana and Michael Kors, along with casual brands such as True Religion and Juicy Couture.

Under the Radar Las Vegas

Vegas is the ultimate urban chameleon, constantly changing to new realities — there's always something exciting to discover. Help keep overtourism in check by going beyond the casinos, clubs and celebrity-driven hotspots along the Strip and connect with local life and surprising sights in lesser-impacted and more down-to-earth areas.

WEICHEN/SHUTTERSTOCK ©

Springs Preserve Soak in some fresh air at this educational museum complex offering an eye-opening romp through local history, culture and biology. (p104)

Burlesque Hall of Fame No need to worship at the altar of hedonism to enjoy this fun and sexy exhibit of 'bump and grind' history and paraphernalia. (p127)

Chinatown Plaza Dim sum to pho and fiery Sichuan noodles are the ammo of Vegas' burgeoning strip of Asian restaurants anchored by a dragon-festooned gate. (p108)

Pinball Hall of Fame Travel back to pre-digital entertainment with this storied collection of historic arcade staples. (p98)

Sunset Drum Circle Bang on the drum to wake up 'The Mantis' at the Downtown Container Park as the sun goes down. (p113)

Flamingo Wildlife Habitat Watch Chilean flamingos preen and African penguins waddle in this surreal jungle retreat right on the Strip. (p75; pictured)

Don't Tell Mama (✆702-207-0788; www.donttell-mama.com; 517 Fremont St E; ⏰8pm-3am Tue-Sun; 🚌Deuce) On weekends join locals at this friendly downtown piano bar to hear their favorite 'singing bartenders' belt out requests. Freeflowing cocktails and no cover.

VegeNation (✆702-366-8515; https://vegenationlv.com; 616 E Carson Ave;

mains $13; ⏰8am-9pm Sun-Thu, to 10pm Fri & Sat; ❄🛜🗲; 🚌Deuce, BHX) Skip the buffet and go healthy with insanely delicious plant-based tacos, sandwiches, pizzas and desserts, all made from local products and served to an adoring local fan base.

Ghost Donkey (www.ghostdonkey.com; Cosmopolitan; ⏰4pm-midnight, to 2am Fri & Sat) Try finding the door to this clandestine mezcal and tequila bar at the Cosmopolitan – it's all part of the fun. (Hint: it's the one under the Exit sign with the donkey on it in Cosmo's food hall.)

Architecture

In Vegas, there's the old and the new, the classic and the cutting edge, the original and the copycat. As a general rule, you'll find the former Downtown and the latter – grandly, gaudily, quite unmistakably – along the Strip. Here are a few highlights from across Vegas' architectural arc.

JAMES MATTIL/SHUTTERSTOCK ©

Replica Architecture

Paris Las Vegas With small-scale versions of the Eiffel Tower and the Arc de Triomphe, this brightly shining behemoth brings Light City to Sin City. (p56)

New York–New York NYNY is the next best thing to actually visiting the Big Apple, thanks to its Statue of Liberty and other replicas. (p46)

Luxor Prepare for your audience with the Sphinx in this giant glass pyramid that shoots out the world's strongest light beam. (p75)

Venetian Sip cappuccino on St Mark's Square amid grand canals and a towering campanile. (p60)

Caesars Palace As outlandish as its namesake, this mini-colosseum brims with Roman statuary, including a 25ft statue of Fortuna. (p73)

Downtown Architecture

El Cortez This heritage-listed 1941 classic is festooned with original neon. (p127; pictured)

Mob Museum Study up on Capone, Bugsy and their fellow mobsters in this neo-classical former courthouse. (p116)

Fremont Street Experience Under the modern frame, a historic theater – El Portal, dating from 1928 – still stands. (p128)

Neon Museum Enter the 'neon boneyard' via the lobby of the La Concha Hotel, a shell-shaped mid-century beauty. (p125)

Edgy Architecture

CityCenter This sleek, blue-glassed complex has to be appreciated for its sheer enormity alone. (p52)

Wynn & Encore Casinos Effortlessly elegant and graceful, these marvels of modern architecture showcase Vegas' design at its best. (p64)

Container Park Urban fashion, art and drinking complex built from shipping containers and festooned with the 'Praying Mantis' sculpture. (p123)

Cosmopolitan Arguably the coolest joint in town, chic Cosmo's fantastic lobby doles out a dose of fun and eye candy galore. (p53)

For Newlyweds

MARK READ/LONELY PLANET ©

Of course, you don't have to elope to find romance in Sin City. Steal a kiss over cocktails at one of the city's sky-high bars, clasp hands as you watch the Bellagio's dancing fountains show, or just hide out with your paramour in a luxury suite all weekend.

Whether or not you're planning to tie the knot, it's no secret that Sin City is practically made for lovers – at least those who don't take themselves too seriously. Room service menus offer champagne, gourmet chocolate and x-rated goodies should you need help to get in the mood. High-end restaurants and bars feature cozy seating and dining areas ideal for a romantic rendezvous, while chapels – both freestanding and located within the resorts – specialize in walk-up weddings, just in case the mood strikes.

Mention to the hotel receptionist that you're on a romantic getaway and you'll be offered add-ons from whirlpool tubs to rose petals strewn across the bed at turndown time. The cheesy 'Just Married' accessories for sale around town aren't just a kitschy souvenir: you're bound to enjoy a few free drinks if you're wearing them when you walk through the Strip's bars and casinos.

Gondola Ride Float along the Venetian's canals, or under a moonlit lake. (p61)

Graceland Wedding Chapel Seal the deal where Jon Bon Jovi did. Elvis impersonator optional. (p128; pictured)

Qua Baths & Spa A gorgeous spa fit for brides-to-be or honeymooners. (p73)

Mandarin Bar & Tea Lounge Toast the future with tea or champagne overlooking the Strip. (p55)

Eiffel Tower Experience Imagine you're honeymooning in the City of Lights. (p57)

Vegas Weddings The only drive-thru wedding window in the city, plus a pretty mini-cathedral. (p128)

Spa by Mandara Couples can opt for the romantic 'Paris for Lovers' treatment package, with a whirlpool tub made for two. (p57)

La Cave At this intimate lair with archways and candlelight, you can pretend you're having tapas and wine in Barcelona. (p76)

Parasol Up & Parasol Down Memorable venues for a romantic rendezvous over artisan cocktails. (p67)

For Kids

Las Vegas may be a bit too sinful to be truly family-friendly. But if you look past the smoke and glitter – which admittedly is hard to do in this town – you'll notice a range of attractions and activities suitable for all ages.

ZIKG/SHUTTERSTOCK ©

Most casinos have virtual-reality and video-game arcades, some have roller coasters and thrill rides, and shows suitable for the entire family abound as well. For a more natural environment, head to the Park or LINQ Promenade, where there's plenty of kid-friendly stuff to do. For eats, look for casino and shopping mall food courts.

Thrills & Rides

Big Apple Roller Coaster Hold onto your hat aboard this Coney Island–style coaster at New York–New York. (p47; pictured)

Adventuredome Get your kicks with thrill rides, rock climbing and bungee jumping in the pink-domed indoor amusement park at Circus Circus. (p74)

Stratosphere Feed your teen with adrenaline on the world's highest thrill rides, 110 stories above the Strip. (p73)

SlotZilla Only for the brave, this zipline is suspended 12 stories above the Fremont Street Experience. (p127)

Shows

Mirage Volcano Visible from the Strip, the faux volcano's molten explosions are entertaining for all ages. (p75)

Fremont Street Experience A five-block pedestrian mall topped by an arched canopy and filled with computer-controlled lights. (p128)

Animal Attraction

Shark Reef Aquarium For an audience with fishy friends, head to this walk-through aquarium teeming with over 2000 exotic submarine beasties. (p43)

Flamingo Wildlife Habitat Prancing flamingos and waddling penguins are among the denizens of this exotic mini-zoo. (p75)

Kid-Friendly Exhibits

Discovery Children's Museum Experiment, paint, study scientific concepts or play dress-up in this colorful interactive play-and-learn space. (p125)

Springs Preserve Detour from the Strip for a breath of fresh air and a fix of eco-conscious design at this educational museum complex. (p104)

Four Perfect Days

Day One

ROIGSLJ/SHUTTERSTOCK ©

Start your day by renting a cabana at **Mandalay Bay Beach** (p43; pictured). Explore the casino: you might return for classy cocktails at **Skyfall Lounge** (p43) or French fine dining at **Rivea** (p80). Walk past **Luxor** (p75) to **New York–New York** (p46), then duck into chic **Cosmopolitan** (p53) to gawk at its huge lobby – but be quick, or you won't make it to **Paris** (p56) for lunch with views of the **Bellagio Fountains** (p39).

Ride one stop at the Bally's & Paris Monorail. Walk north to the unmissable **High Roller** (p51). Take a ride, or walk the fun **LINQ Promenade** (p50). If you fancy a first flutter, try **LINQ** (p72). Cross the street to **Caesars Palace** (p73) for dinner and a show.

After dinner, hit **Drai's** (p85), if you're appropriately attired. Tip: swap walking between stops with rides on the Deuce/SDX buses.

Day Two

MATTEO_IT/SHUTTERSTOCK ©

Head to **Aria** (p53) to admire the eclectic **CityCenter fine art collection** (p53). Pop next door to the **Shops at Crystals** (p88) or back to **Cosmopolitan** (p53) to further explore this playground of the nouveau riches. Take note of the **Chandelier Lounge** (p85; pictured) for cocktails later. Walk north past **Paris Las Vegas** (p56) and the **Venetian** (p60) to the latter's sophisticated little sister, **Palazzo** (p63).

Walk across the skybridge to Steve Wynn's signature showpiece, **Wynn** (p64). Stroll through the sumptuous atrium, stopping at the whimsical **Parasol Up Parasol Down** (p67) to gaze upon the Lake of Dreams, then cross the casino floor to **Encore** (p64) and check with the concierge for last-minute tickets to Cirque du Soleil's underwater masterpiece, **Le Rêve the Dream** (p65).

KIT LEONG/SHUTTERSTOCK ©

Day Three

Head to the western corner of N Las Vegas Blvd and Fremont St to explore Downtown, where it all began. Ride the **Slotzilla** (p127; pictured) zipline or walk the length of Fremont St to the iconic **Golden Nugget** (p114) with its shark tank and largest gold nugget ever found. Opposite, you'll find antique **Binion's** (p126) – a must for Elvis fans! Continue north to Stewart Ave and the **Mob Museum** (p116) to learn how the Mafia shaped Sin City. Grab a taxi to the **Neon Museum** (avoid walking as it's not the best part of town). After, head to the **Burlesque Hall of Fame** (p127), then get a shot of **El Cortez** (p127), opposite, and continue a block east to the quirky **Container Park** (p113). Kick off the evening at the speakeasy-style **Downtown Cocktail Room** (p130) or the rooftop patio at **Commonwealth** (p119).

KIT LEONG/SHUTTERSTOCK ©

Day Four

Start by heading west of the Strip to family-friendly **Springs Preserve** (p104; pictured) to explore Sin City's natural and cultural side, then on to the **Rio** (p108) to woosh 400ft in the air on the **VooDoo Zipline** (p108). Stay at the Rio to feast at the **Carnival World Buffet** (p110) or head to for noodle soups or barbecue at **Chinatown Plaza** (p108).

Head east of the Strip to see the fascinating **National Atomic Testing Museum** (p94) to learn about the early nuclear age. Take a trip to the **Pinball Hall of Fame** (p98) or make your way to **Firefly** (p98) for happy hour drinks.

Hit the show at the **The Theater** (p101) or get a dose of hilarious madness at the **Double Down Saloon** (p100).

Need to Know

For detailed information, see Survival Guide (p143)

Currency
US dollar ($)

Language
English

Visas
Not usually required for citizens of Canada or the 38 Visa Waiver Program countries with ESTA pre-authorization.

Money
ATM transaction fees in casino gaming areas are high. Credit cards are widely accepted.

Cell Phones
Cell phones must be a multiband GSM model.

Time
Pacific Time Zone (GMT/UTC minus eight hours)

Tipping
Fifteen percent doesn't cut it anymore. The standard tip is 18% to 20% of the bill. If a service charge has already been included (usually for groups of six or more), don't tip twice. At buffets, leave a couple of dollars per person on the table.

Daily Budget

Budget: Less than $100
Downtown casino hotel room: $30–80
Takeout meal: $6–12
24-hour RTC bus pass: $8

Midrange: $100–250
Standard Strip casino hotel room: $65–150
Discounted show ticket: $30–90
Casual restaurant meal: $20–45
24-hour self-parking at a Strip hotel: $10–15

Top end: More than $250
Luxury Strip hotel suite: $200-plus
VIP show ticket: $125-plus
Celebrity-chef dining: $100-plus

Useful Websites

Lonely Planet (www.lonelyplanet.com/usa/las-vegas) Destination information, hotel bookings, traveler forum and more.
Las Vegas Tourism (www.lasvegastourism.com) Official website of Las Vegas Tourism.
Las Vegas Weekly (www.lasvegasweekly.com) Popular weekly magazine with listings, in print and online.

Advance Planning

One month before Book flights, a hotel and a rental car for trips out of town.

Three weeks before Score tickets for production shows, mega-concerts or headliner events.

One week before Book a table at a happening chef's restaurant or an outdoor adventure tour.

Arriving in Las Vegas

Most travelers arrive in Las Vegas by car or by plane.

✈ McCarran International Airport

The airport is located relatively close to the Strip. Shuttle buses depart for casino hotels around the clock; these cost from $7 one-way to Strip hotels, and from $9 to Downtown and off-Strip hotels. Taxis are readily available. You'll pay at least $20 plus tip for a taxi to the Strip – tell your driver to use surface streets, not the I-15 Fwy airport connector tunnel ('long-hauling').

🚗 Driving

Most travelers approach the Strip (Las Vegas Blvd) off the I-15 Fwy. Try to avoid exiting onto busy Flamingo Rd; opt for quieter Tropicana Ave or Spring Mountain Rd.

Getting Around

The Strip is miles long: you can walk between some casino resorts, but you'll need a ride to reach others, or to go downtown. Driving on the Strip can be stressful.

🚌 Bus

Deuce buses to/from downtown stop every block or two along the Strip. SDX express buses stop at some Strip casino hotels and at some off-Strip shopping malls.

Rideshare

Uber and Lyft are by far the best way to get around Vegas in most circumstances.

Shuttle

Many off-Strip casino hotels offer shuttle buses to and from the Strip, although some are reserved for hotel guests. A free public shuttle connects the Rio with Harrah's and Bally's/Paris Las Vegas.

🚕 Taxi

There are taxi stands at almost every casino hotel and shopping mall. Rides cost at least $20, plus tip.

🚋 Tram

Free trams operate on three routes connecting casino resorts.

Las Vegas Neighborhoods

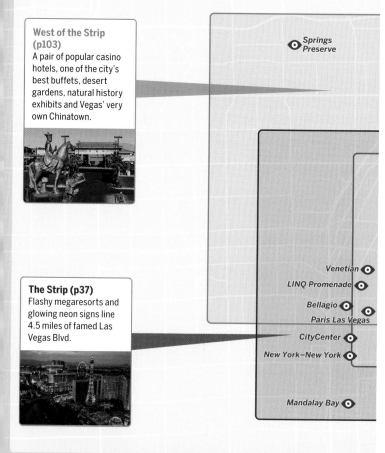

West of the Strip (p103)
A pair of popular casino hotels, one of the city's best buffets, desert gardens, natural history exhibits and Vegas' very own Chinatown.

The Strip (p37)
Flashy megaresorts and glowing neon signs line 4.5 miles of famed Las Vegas Blvd.

Springs Preserve

Venetian
LINQ Promenade
Bellagio
Paris Las Vegas
CityCenter
New York–New York

Mandalay Bay

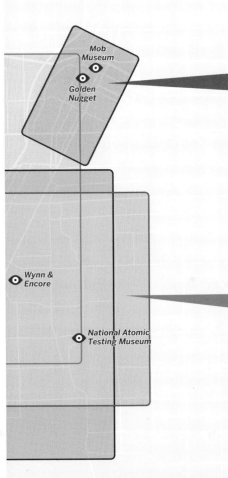

Mob
Museum

Golden
Nugget

Wynn &
Encore

National Atomic
Testing Museum

Downtown & Fremont Street (p113)
Vintage Vegas vibes, old-school casinos, excellent new museums and a burgeoning hipster nightlife scene in Sin City's Downtown.

East of the Strip (p93)
Quirky special-interest museums, university bars, secondhand shopping and a perennially cool rock 'n' roll–themed resort.

Explore
Las Vegas

Fremont Street (p113) APRILPIX/500PX ©

Explore ◈
The Strip

The 4.2-mile Strip (a section of S Las Vegas Blvd) is what happens when you take the ideals of freedom and abundance to their extremes. It's Vegas' entertainment central, the epicenter in a vortex of limitless potential, where almost anything goes and time becomes elastic.

The Short List

o **Bellagio (p38)** *Being mesmerized by the dancing fountains.*

o **LINQ Promenade (p50)** *Escaping the desert heat with a stroll down the LINQ Promenade, with its fun boutiques, pubs and eateries, and the world's largest Ferris wheel.*

o **Paris Las Vegas (p56)** *Visiting America's version of the 'City of Light'.*

o **Stratosphere (p72)** *Enjoying the knockout views and selection of heart-stopping, sky-high rides at Nevada's tallest building.*

o **Caesars Palace (p73)** *Wandering around Vegas' homage to the decadence of ancient Rome.*

Getting There & Around

🚶 The Strip is 4.2 miles long – don't assume you can walk easily between casino hotels, even those that appear to be close together.

🚌 Day passes on the 24-hour Deuce and faster (though not 24-hour and not servicing all casinos) SDX buses are an excellent way to get around.

Ride-share Ride-share where possible – rates are great and you'll never wait long.

Neighborhood Map on p70

The Las Vegas Strip KRIS DAVIDSON/LONELY PLANET ©

Top Experience 📷
Enjoy the Opulence at Bellagio

Inspired by the beauty of a lakeside Italian village, casino magnate Steve Wynn's original Vegas pleasure palazzo, with its ornate Tuscan architecture and artificial lake, anchors the center Strip. A thousand dancing fountains spring from the lake's waters and, while its overt opulence can be too much for some, Bellagio's secret delight is that romance is always in the air.

◎ MAP P70, C5

📞 702-693-7111

www.bellagio.com

3600 S Las Vegas Blvd

🕐 24hr

P

🚌 Deuce

Fountains of Bellagio

Out of the faux Italian lake spring the dancing **Fountains of Bellagio** (www.bellagio.com; 3600 S Las Vegas Blvd, Bellagio; admission free; ⏲ shows every 30min 3-7pm Mon-Fri, noon-7pm Sat, 2:30-7pm Sun, every 15min 7pm-midnight Mon-Sat, 11am-2:30pm & 7pm-midnight Sun; P ♿; 🚌 Deuce), every 15 to 30 minutes throughout the afternoon and evening. The recorded soundtrack varies; if you're lucky, it'll be Italian opera or ol' Blue Eyes crooning 'Luck Be a Lady.' For front-row seats, head to Hyde for happy hour and lean over the balcony to almost feel the spray, or reserve an outdoor patio table at one of Bellagio's lakefront restaurants. Afterward, stroll over to Jean Philippe Patisserie, just so you can say you've seen the world's largest chocolate fountain up close.

Lobby

The hotel's gasp-worthy lobby has an 18ft-high ceiling adorned with a backlit glass sculpture by Dale Chihuly, comprised of 2000 hand-blown flowers in vibrant colors. It's especially lovely to behold when someone is playing the grand piano at the nearby **Petrossian Bar** (📞 702-693-7111; https://bellagio.mgmresorts.com; Bellagio; ⏲ 24hr).

Bellagio Conservatory & Botanical Gardens

At the **Bellagio Conservatory & Botanical Gardens** (www.bellagio.com; 3600 S Las Vegas Blvd, Bellagio; admission free; ⏲ 24hr; P ♿; 🚌 Deuce), ostentatious seasonal floral arrangements are installed by cranes through the soaring 50ft ceiling. The effect is unnatural, but that doesn't stop crowds from gawking – and the aroma of fresh blooms is truly enchanting. Real flowers, cultivated in a gigantic on-site greenhouse, brighten countless vases throughout the property. Also look around the periphery of the conservatory for classic paintings recreated with buds and blooms instead of oil paint.

★ **Top Tips**

o For the best photo ops of the famous Conservatory, come by in the early morning.

o Checking in? Splurge on a fountain-view room.

o Unaccompanied children under 18 are not allowed at the Bellagio. Baby strollers are prohibited except for use by hotel guests.

✕ **Take a Break**

To enjoy the spectacle of the Fountains of Bellagio over a cold beer, head to **Beer Park** (by Budweiser) (p57).

If you want fine dining with your fountains, set your sights high upon the **Eiffel Tower Restaurant** (p57), or, to get really up-close-and-personal, **Todd English's Olives** (p82).

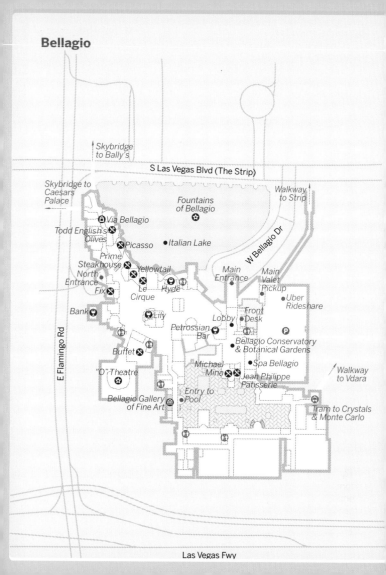

Bellagio Gallery of Fine Art

Since Steve Wynn sold his baby to the MGM Grand group for $6.4 billion, Bellagio hasn't been blessed with the same world-class art. Yet its petite **fine arts gallery** (☎702-693-7871; www.bellagio.com; 3600 S Las Vegas Blvd, Bellagio; adult/child under 12yr $16/free; ☉10am-8pm, last entry 7:30pm; 🅿️🚻; 🚍Deuce) still hosts such blockbuster traveling shows as Claude Monet: Impressions of Light and American Modernism from the Museum of Fine Arts, Boston. Original modern art masterworks hang inside **Picasso** (☎702-693-8865; https://bellagio.mgmresorts.com; Bellagio; prix-fixe dinner menus with/without wine pairings $179/119; ☉5-9:30pm Wed-Mon; 🍴) restaurant, nearby.

Pool Complex

Sprawling behind the hotel, Bellagio's lushly landscaped five-pool complex evokes the Mediterranean. As only hotel guests are able to experience it, and no unaccompanied children under 14 years old are allowed, it's also a relatively tranquil pool scene for Vegas. To unwind even more, hotel guests can book rejuvenating treatments at **Spa Bellagio** (☎702-693-7472; Bellagio; guests/nonguests day pass $50/100; ☉7am-7pm).

Cirque du Soleil's 'O'

Phonetically speaking, it's the French word for water (eau). With a lithe international cast performing

Steve Wynn's Vision

Steve Wynn dreamed up the $1.6 billion Bellagio, adorned with $300 million worth of art from his personal collection of masterpieces. Built on the ashes of the demolished 1950s-era Dunes, Bellagio was one of the world's most opulent casino hotels when it opened in 1998. It also brought a surprising touch of elegance to Sin City, which had become infamous for its down-and-dirty strip clubs and low-class culture. Wynn sold the Mirage and Bellagio megaresorts to business rival MGM Grand in 2000.

in, on and above water, **O** (☎702-693-8866; www.cirquedusoleil.com/o; 3600 S Las Vegas Blvd, Bellagio; tickets $90-215; ☉7pm & 9:30pm; 🚻; 🚍Deuce) is a spectacular feat of imagination and engineering, and you'll pay dearly to see it – the company never sells discounted tickets.

Jean Philippe Patisserie

As certified by the *Guinness Book of World Records*, the world's largest chocolate fountain cascades inside the front windows of this champion pastry-maker's shop, known for its fantastic sorbets, gelati, pastries and chocolate confections. Coffee and espresso are above the Strip's low-bar average.

Top Experience 📷

Be Dazzled by Glittering Mandalay Bay

Angular and glittering, massive Mandalay Bay flanks the far south end of the Strip. It's the first resort many visitors lay eyes on as they roll into Las Vegas – and what better introduction to Sin City than this gleaming tropics-themed, high-rise shrine to casino gaming and high-rolling, with its massive beach, aquarium, exceptional dining and two luxe hotels-within-a-hotel.

◎ MAP P70, C8

📞 702-632-7700

www.mandalaybay.com

3950 S Las Vegas Blvd

🕐 24hr

🅿 🚻

🚌 Deuce

Mandalay Bay Beach

The 1.6-million-gallon wave pool at **Mandalay Bay Beach** (☏702-632-4760; www.mandalaybay.com/en/amenities/beach.html; 3950 S Las Vegas Blvd, Mandalay Bay; hotel guests free, nonguests adult/child $20/10; ⏱pool 8am-7pm, Moorea Beach Club from 10am; ⓅⓀ) occupies 11 acres, has 2700 tons of imported Californian sand and can generate waves up to 6ft. The facility also includes a lazy river (kids love it) and the 'top-tional' adults-only **Moorea Beach Club**. Access is complimentary for resort guests. Nonguests can enjoy the facilities by renting a reserved seat ($50 to $75 daily), daybed (from $225) or cabana ($300 to $600); daybeds and cabanas can be used by four to 10 people.

Skyfall Lounge

One of M-Bay's lesser-known draw-cards is the fabulous, dress-to-impress **Skyfall Lounge** (☏702-632-7575; www.delanolasvegas.com; Delano; ⏱5pm-midnight Sun-Thu, to 1am Fri & Sat), atop the Delano hotel, from where you can enjoy unparalleled views of the southern Strip and sip cocktails as the sun sets over the spectacular Spring Mountains. The bar's classy, subdued vibe becomes ever so slightly more tactile when top DJs start spinning mellow beats after dark and the more self-assured (or inebriated) guests get primed to dance the night away.

Shark Reef Aquarium

Adults, kids and lovers of marine life flock to Mandalay Bay for its unique and unusual walk-through **Shark Reef Aquarium** (☏702-632-4555; www.sharkreef.com; 3950 S Las Vegas Blvd; adult/child $22/15; ⏱10am-8pm Sun-Thu, to 10pm Fri & Sat; ⓅⓀ). Here you'll find around 2000 species of submarine critters, including jellyfish, moray eels, stingrays and, of course, several species of shark. Also on display are some of the world's last remaining golden crocodiles. Scuba-diver caretakers and naturalists are available to chat as you wander around.

★ Top Tips

○ Free trams shuttle between Mandalay Bay and the Luxor and Excalibur casino hotels.

○ Pick up tickets for an outdoor concert by the Mandalay Bay Beach swimming pool at the Mandalay Bay Events Center (p45).

○ Shop around for discounted tickets to Michael Jackson ONE (p45) – bargains can be found.

✗ Take a Break

Take a stroll through the airy **Shoppes at Mandalay Place** (☏702-632-7700; www.mandalaybay.com; Mandalay Bay; ⏱10am-11pm) promenade for coffee and window-shopping.

If it's hot outside, cool off with icy cocktails inside **Minus5 Ice Bar** (☏702-740-5800; www.minus5experience.com; Shoppes at Mandalay Place; entry with parka, gloves & boot rental $17, incl 1 cocktail $45; ⏱11am-2am Sun-Thu, to 3am Fri & Sat).

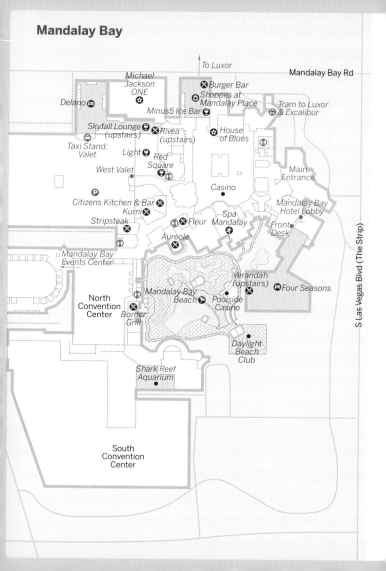

Mandalay Bay

To Luxor

Mandalay Bay Rd

Michael Jackson ONE

Burger Bar

Shoppes at Mandalay Place

Delano

Minus5 Ice Bar

Tram to Luxor & Excalibur

Skyfall Lounge (upstairs)

Rivea (upstairs)

House of Blues

Taxi Stand; Valet

Light

Red Square

West Valet

Casino

Main Entrance

Citizens Kitchen & Bar

Kumi

Fleur

Spa Mandalay

Mandalay Bay Hotel Lobby

Stripsteak

Aureole

Front Desk

Mandalay Bay Events Center

Verandah (upstairs)

Four Seasons

North Convention Center

Mandalay Bay Beach

Poolside Casino

Border Grill

Daylight Beach Club

Shark Reef Aquarium

South Convention Center

S Las Vegas Blvd (The Strip)

The History of M-Bay

The 1950s-era Hacienda resort was imploded in 1996 to clear the way for Mandalay Bay. The resort's upscale tropical theme may be subtle, but its grand opening – during which Jim Belushi, Dan Aykroyd and John Goodman cruised through the front doors on motorcycles – certainly wasn't. Today, a Harley-Davidson crew might look out of place in the regal, ivory-hued lobby.

Michael Jackson ONE

Disco babes flock to M-Bay to relive their favorite moments from the 'King of Pop's' almost 40-year career at Cirque du Soleil's musical homage to this peerless legend, **Michael Jackson ONE** (702-632-7580; www.cirquedusoleil. com/michael-jackson-one; Mandalay Bay; tickets from $69; 7pm & 9:30pm Thu-Mon). Featuring showstopping dancers, lissome acrobats and aerialists all moving to a soundtrack of MJ's greatest hits, the show moon-walks all the way back to his break-out platinum album, *Thriller*. No children under five years old allowed. You don't have to stay at the Bay to see the show, but it sure adds another great reason to, if you needed further persuasion.

House of Blues

In the **House of Blues** (702-632-7600; www.houseofblues.com; Mandalay Bay; box office 9am-9pm), the sophisticated **Foundation Room** (702-632-7601; www.houseofblues. com; Mandalay Bay; cover usually $30; 5pm-2am) nightclub hosts nightly DJ parties and special events in a stylish space that's half Gothic mansion, half Hindu temple. The expansive views of the Strip are as impressive as the decor. Look for club promoters around the casino passing out two-for-one drink and free-entry tickets. But if club-bing's not your bag, perhaps the legendary **House of Blues Gospel Brunch** (702-632-7600; www. houseofblues.com/lasvegas; Mandalay Bay; adult/child under 11yr $54/27; seatings 10am & 1pm Sun;) on Sundays will be. Here, Saturday-night sinners can find redemption over unlimited Bloody Marys and Southern and soul-food favorites such as jambalaya, chicken and waffles, jalapeño cornbread and warm banana-bread pudding. Mmm-mmm!

Mandalay Bay Events Center

Operatic tenor Luciano Pavarotti performed at the opening of this arena-style **events center** (702-632-7777; www.mandalaybay. com; Mandalay Bay; box office 10am-6pm), which hosts championship boxing, ultimate fighting and headliner concerts from Journey to Lady Antebellum.

Top Experience 📷
Explore New York in Miniature

Make no mistake: with its miniature replica skyline and themed bars, New York-New York is nothing like the Big Apple – except for the fact that, like its namesake, it isn't exactly wholesome. Still, the Vegas version, with its eye-catching monuments such as a pint-sized Statue of Liberty, a scaled-down Brooklyn Bridge and a Coney Island–style roller coaster, is good-spirited fun.

◉ MAP P70, C7

☑ 800-689-1797

www.newyorknewyork.com

3790 S Las Vegas Blvd

🕐 24hr

P

NYC- Inspired Architecture

The mini-megalopolis of New York–New York features scaled-down replicas of the Big Apple's landmarks, such as the Statue of Liberty and a miniature Brooklyn Bridge out front. Rising above are perspective-warping replicas of the Chrysler, Empire State and Bankers Trust buildings. Inside, don't overlook the bas-relief map of the USA or Greenwich Village's cobblestone streets.

Big Apple Arcade & Roller Coaster

The gargantuan **Big Apple Arcade** (New York–New York; ⏰8am-midnight; 🅿🚻) boasts 200-plus video games ranging from '80s classics to the latest Japanese imports. It leads out to the Coney Island–inspired **Roller Coaster** (☎702-740-6616; New York–New York; s ride/day pass $15/26; ⏰10:30am-midnight; 🅿🚻), ridden by more than a million people each year and known for its twist-and-dive maneuver, which produces a sensation similar to that a fighter pilot feels during a barrel roll. The rest of the three-minute trip includes stomach-dropping dips, high-banked turns, a 180-degree spiral and blink-and-you'll-miss-it views of the Strip. Hold on tight: your head, back and shoulders will take a beating on this bumpy ride. All riders must be at least 54in tall.

Nine Fine Irishmen

Built in Ireland and shipped piece by piece to America, the **Nine Fine Irishmen** (☎702-740-6463; https://newyorknewyork.mgmresorts.com; New York–New York; ⏰11am-11pm Mon-Fri, from 9am Sat & Sun; 📶; 🚌Deuce) pub has cavernous interior booths and outdoor patio tables beside the Brooklyn Bridge. Live entertainment is a mix of Celtic rock and traditional Irish country tunes, occasionally with sing-alongs and a champion Irish dancer. Dig into finessed country cooking from this decent (though pricey) menu of lamb stew, bangers and mash, corned-beef sandwiches and other pub

★ Top Tips

o The crowd here is mostly young and party-hearty, not Upper East Side–elegant.

o The roller coaster is especially thrilling at night: it stays open until 11pm Sunday to Thursday, and until 12am on weekends.

o Staying the night? These digs are decent, but rather tiny – best for fun-loving budget travelers.

✕ Take a Break

Bar at Times Square (☎702-740-6466; https://newyorknewyork.mgmresorts.com; New York–New York; cover $15-25, free until 8pm; ⏰1pm-2:30am Mon-Thu, from 11am Fri-Sun, live music 8pm-2am) is famous for its dueling piano acts.

Grab a slice at **New York Pizzeria** (☎702-736-7111; https://newyorknewyork.mgmresorts.com; New York–New York; pizza & snacks $4-14; ⏰10am-1am Sun-Thu, to 4am Fri & Sat; 🚻) or sip North American microbrews at **Pour 24** (p49).

New York–New York

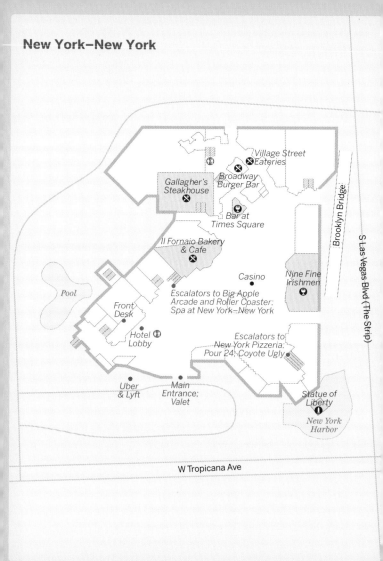

grub, washed down with pints of Guinness. Vegetarians aren't totally left out, with herb-crusted goat cheese salad, baked brie with oven-roasted tomatoes and fried pickles on the menu.

Pour 24

Upstairs next to the skybridge entrance, **Pour 24** (☎702-740-6969; https://newyorknewyork.mgmresorts. com; New York–New York; ☻24hr) looks like just any other standard casino bar. The draw is the long list of American craft beers – like Dogfish Head's 60 Minute IPA and Big Sky's Moose Drool – on draft and in bottles, or create your own tasting flight.

Gallagher's Steak house

This reproduction of a classy NYC **steakhouse** (☎702-740-6450; https://newyorknewyork.mgmresorts. com; New York–New York; mains $28-52; ☻4-11pm, to midnight Fri & Sat) – the original Gallagher's dates from 1927 – drums up a serious dinner menu with lobster bisque, wedge salads, dry-aged bone-in sirloin (the house specialty, which you'll see hanging in glass-fronted meat lockers out front) and side dishes like housemade potato chips. The circular bar is an atmospheric spot for a martini with your bros.

New York in Sin City

With a price tag of $460 million, New York–New York opened in 1997. A few years later, after the terrorist attacks of September 11, 2001, spontaneous tributes – predominantly T-shirts from police and fire companies around the nation – started pouring into the Vegas resort. These were displayed for more than a decade, a sort of impromptu monument, in front of New York–New York's Lady Liberty statue.

Il Fornaio Bakery & Cafe

Take a bite of wood-fired pizza, pasta and salads at this classic NY-style Italian **joint** (☎702-650-6500; www.ilfornaio.com/lasvegas; New York–New York; mains from $20; ☻7am-11pm, to midnight Fri-Sun). House specialties include lasagna layered with porcini mushrooms; cannelloni stuffed with rotisserie chicken, organic spinach and smoked mozzarella; and spicy linguine tossed with clams, mussels, prawns and scallops. Gourmet omelets bring out the breakfast crowd.

Top Experience 📸
Wander the LINQ Promenade

A mammoth open-air dining, entertainment and retail complex, the $550-million LINQ project has transformed the once-lackluster stretch of the center Strip between the vintage Flamingo and rebranded LINQ casino hotels. Eclectic shops, buzzing bars, trendy restaurants, live-music venues and even a bowling alley line the pedestrian LINQ Promenade. Above it all rises the landmark High Roller observation wheel.

◉ MAP P70, C5

☏ 800-634-6441

www.caesars.com/linq

3545 S Las Vegas Blvd

🕑 24hr

🅿 👫

🚌 Deuce, 🚈 Harrah's/The Linq

High Roller

The world's largest observation wheel, the
High Roller (☏ 702-322-0593; www.caesars.
com/linq/high-roller; 3545 S Las Vegas Blvd, LINQ
Promenade; adult/child $25/10, after 5pm $37/20;
⏱11:30am-2am; P 🚻; 🚌Deuce, 🚌Harrah's/
Linq), towers 550ft above the LINQ's street-
level walkways. Each of the 28 air-conditioned
passenger cabins is enclosed by handcrafted
Italian glass. Outside, 2000 colorful LED lights
glow from dusk until dawn. One revolution
takes about 30 minutes, and you'll be sharing
the ride with a few dozen strangers. Since
this is Vegas, the wheelhouse bar sells boozy
drinks to take on board.

Brooklyn Bowl

Brooklyn Bowl (☏ 702-862-2695; www.brooklyn
bowl.com/las-vegas; LINQ Promenade; 30min lane
rental from $20, show tickets free-$70; ⏱5pm-late)
is a kind of hybridized high-tech bowling alley/
comfort-food-meets-gourmet restaurant and
killer concert venue for the kind of indie su-
perbands you'd hear headlining the Coachella
or SXSW music festivals.

Virgil's Real BBQ

If you've never tried real-deal Southern
cooking, and you're not shy of chunks of
mouthwatering smoky meats, baby back ribs,
cheesy grits and sugary caramelized sides,
you simply must make a beeline for **Virgil's
Real BBQ** (☏ 702-389-7400; www.virgilsbbq.com;
LINQ Promenade; mains $10-28; ⏱8am-midnight,
to 1am Fri & Sat).

★ Top Tips

○ From 4pm to 7pm,
select pods on the
High Roller host the
adults-only (21-plus)
'happy half hour' with
an open bar (read
all-you-can-drink)
shared between your
fellow riders.

○ The southwest
corner of each High
Roller pod affords
the best views of the
Strip (that's to the
right of the door as
you enter).

○ LINQ's casino (p72),
including its lovingly
reinvented O'Sheas
pub casino, is a great
place for a first flutter.

✕ Take a Break

For quick bites,
head to **Jaburrito,**
(☏ 702-901-7375; www.
jaburritos.com; LINQ
Promenade; items $10-
13; ⏱11am-11pm Sun-
Thu, to midnight Fri &
Sat) where sushi rolls
make food love to
the humble burrito,
or **Gordon Ram-
say Fish & Chips**
(☏ 702-322-0529;
www.gordonramsayres-
taurants.com/gordon-
ramsay-fish-chips; LINQ
Promenade; meals from
$16; ⏱11am-10pm).

Top Experience 📸

Admire Art and Architecture at CityCenter

Say goodbye kitschy themes and say hello to sleek lines. Traditionally, themed Strip hotels competed to outdo each other, but CityCenter changed the game by refusing to compete at all. This mini-'city' of cutting-edge hotels, restaurants and designer boutiques is a towering luxury playground, whose design smarts and art have transformed the Strip's skyline and cultural landscape.

◎ MAP P70, C6

www.aria.com

3780 S Las Vegas Blvd

P

🚌 Deuce, 🚋 Crystals

Shops at Crystals

The structure of CityCenter's dazzling shopping mall (p88) is an architectural and cultural attraction in its own right. Admire the angular glass canopy jutting onto Las Vegas Blvd, then walk inside to find a three-story 'treehouse' made of smooth, dark wood, as well as a kid-friendly, high-tech art installation composed of neon tube lights and glass-encased funnels of swirling water.

Fine Art Collection

Worth more than $40 million, CityCenter's thought-provoking **fine art collection** (☎702-590-7111; www.aria.com; 3730 S Las Vegas Blvd; admission free; ⏰24hr; P; 🚌Deuce, 🚋Crystals) is freely displayed throughout the complex's public spaces. You can pick up a self-guided brochure from hotel and shopping mall concierge desks or download a free mobile walking tour app, but the real appeal is stumbling on unexpected works around every corner.

Cosmopolitan

The Strip's hippest casino resort for now, **Cosmo** (☎702-698-7000; www.cosmopolitanlasvegas.com; 3708 S Las Vegas Blvd; ⏰24hr; P; 🚌Deuce) avoids utter pretension, despite the constant wink-wink, arty-retro flourishes such as the Art-o-Mats (vintage cigarette machines hawking original art rather than nicotine), the help-yourself pool tables surrounded by old-school leather armchairs and the larger-than-life red stiletto heel that you can climb into for a tongue-in-cheek Vegas photo op.

Aria

CityCenter's architectural showpiece, **Aria** (☎702-590-7111; www.aria.com; 3730 S Las Vegas Blvd, CityCenter; ⏰24hr; P) centers on a sophisticated casino accented with sleek chrome, polished stone and dark wood. It's a

★ Top Tips

○ Even if you can't afford to stay here, don't be shy! Be sure to have a wander around Cosmopolitan's fabulous lobby and casino floor and take a look at the free Fine Art Collection.

○ Cosmopolitan has a 'secret' (unlisted) pizza joint that makes delicious pies. You can find the details pretty easily online, but if in doubt, ask the concierge.

✗ Take a Break

For classy small plates, Cosmopolitan's **China Poblano** (p78), surprisingly, fuses Chinese and Mexican cuisine remarkably well.

Alternatively, stop for a drink at the designer drool-worthy **Chandelier Lounge** (p85) or Aria's Lobby Bar.

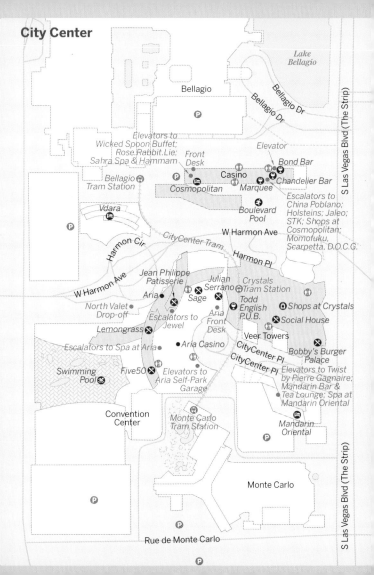

City Center

Lake Bellagio

Bellagio

Bellagio Dr

Bellagio Dr

S Las Vegas Blvd (The Strip)

Elevator

Elevators to Wicked Spoon Buffet; Rose.Rabbit.Lie; Sahra Spa & Hammam

Front Desk

Bond Bar

Casino

Chandelier Bar

Bellagio Tram Station

Cosmopolitan

Marquee

Escalators to China Poblano; Holsteins; Jaleo; STK; Shops at Cosmopolitan; Momofuku, Scarpetta, D.O.C.G.

Vdara

Boulevard Pool

Harmon Cir

CityCenter Tram

W Harmon Ave

Harmon Pl

W Harmon Ave

Jean Philippe Patisserie

Julian Serrano

Crystals Tram Station

Aria

Sage

Shops at Crystals

North Valet Drop-off

Todd English P.U.B.

Social House

Escalators to Jewel

Aria Front Desk

Veer Towers

Lemongrass

Escalators to Spa at Aria

Aria Casino

CityCenter Pl

CityCenter Pl

Bobby's Burger Palace

Five50

Elevators to Aria Self-Park Garage

Elevators to Twist by Pierre Gagnaire; Mandarin Bar & Tea Lounge; Spa at Mandarin Oriental

Swimming Pool

Convention Center

Monte Carlo Tram Station

Mandarin Oriental

Monte Carlo

Rue de Monte Carlo

fitting backdrop for visually stunning restaurants, many run by top chefs. Energy-efficient design features and eco-conscious amenities come as standard benefits, whether you find them at the East-meets-West spa or inside your own cocoon-like hotel room or suite.

Mandarin Oriental & Vdara

Despite all its frenetic energy, CityCenter also enfolds two hushed oases, the **Mandarin Oriental** and all-suites **Vdara** (📞702-590-2111; www.vdara.com; 2600 W Harmon Ave, Aria Campus; ste weekday/weekend from $99/159; 🅿️😋❄️@📶🏊🐾; 🚌Deuce, 🚌Bellagio) hotels, where you can get away from the ding-ding-ding of the slot machines. Even if you're not staying overnight, ride the elevator to the Mandarin Oriental's 23rd-floor 'sky lobby' to take in nighttime views of the Strip's neon lights while you sip champagne cocktails.

Twist by Pierre Gagnaire

If romantic **Twist's** (📞702-590-8888; www.waldorfastorialasvegas.com; Waldorf Astoria, CityCenter; mains $67-76, tasting menus $170-295; 🕐5:30-10pm Tue-Sat, from 6pm Fri & Sat) sparkling nighttime Strip views don't make you gasp, the modern French cuisine by this three-star Michelin chef just might. Seasonal tasting menus at this Mandarin Oriental outpost may include squid-ink gnocchetti topped with carrot gelée or langoustine with grapefruit fondue, finished off with bubble-gum ice cream with marshmallow and green-tea crumbles. Reservations essential; dress code is business casual.

Todd English P.U.B.

Twice-daily happy hours (3pm to 6pm, and 10pm until midnight) with half-price pints and cheap wings, oysters and sliders keep bar stools filled at this cozy brick-walled pub with an outdoor patio. The kitchen closes at 11:30pm daily.

Top Experience 📷
Climb the Eiffel Tower

Paris Las Vegas aims to emulate the essence of the grand dame by recreating her most famous landmarks, including the Eiffel Tower, Arc de Triomphe and Maritime Fountain from the Place de la Concorde. Somehow, here on the Las Vegas Strip, it succeeds in evoking a sense of the City of Light – right down to the accordion players.

◉ MAP P70, C5

📞 877-796-2096

www.caesars.com/paris-las-vegas

3655 S Las Vegas Blvd

🕐 24hr

P ⚥

🚌 Deuce

Eiffel Tower Experience

Families and lovers flock to Vegas' **Eiffel Tower Experience** (📞888-727-4758; www.caesars.com; Paris Las Vegas; adult/child $17/10, after 7pm $22/20; ⏰10am-1am, weather permitting; 🅿♿), lining up for grated views from a windblown observation deck. It's cheaper to take a ride on the tower's elevators during the day, but nighttime panoramas of the Strip, when casino neons blink and flicker and the Bellagio's dancing fountains are illuminated, are worth the marginally extra expense.

Eiffel Tower Restaurant

With all of Vegas' high-end and celebrity dining to choose from, it might feel a bit cheesy to dine at a theme-park-ish replica of the planet's ultimate symbol of romance, but don't be too quick to judge: the ruse is convincing. At this haute **restaurant** (📞702-948-6937; www.eiffeltowerrestaurant.com; Paris Las Vegas; mains lunch $19-36, dinner $38-89; ⏰11:30am-10:30pm Mon-Fri, from 10am Sat & Sun) midway up its namesake tower, the Francophile wine list is vast, the chocolate soufflé is unforgettable, and views of the Strip and Bellagio's fountains are breathtaking. Lunch is your best bet, but it's more popular to come at sunset. Reservations essential.

Beer Park

Occupying a prime spot beneath Paris' Eiffel Tower, **Beer Park (by Budweiser)** (📞702-444-4500; www.beerpark.com; Paris Las Vegas; ⏰11am-2am Mon-Fri, from 9am Sat & Sun) is an open-air beer garden overlooking the Fountains of Bellagio. With tap varieties from around the world and a friendly, easy vibe, it's a cinch to meet other travelers or lovers of the amber liquid. But be warned: it's also an easy spot to get lazy!

Spa by Mandara

At this full-service salon and spa, which mixes Balinese and European influences, the most luxurious treatment rooms have handcrafted

★ Top Tips

○ If you don't have the cash to enjoy dining at the Eiffel Tower, or even riding to the observation deck, one of the best free hangs for watching Bellagio's dancing fountains is Beer Park. Do the right thing, though, and buy one beer, at least.

○ The best spots for photographing the Eiffel Tower are found by making like a tree and cozy-ing up to the trunks across the Strip, adjacent to Bellagio's Lake Como.

✗ Take a Break

You can't go past **Beer Park** for a casual, relaxed place to rest your weary legs, take in the surroundings and enjoy a cold beer or light meal.

If you just need a quick, cheap feed (sans views), head around the corner for Cali-Japanese ramen at **Ramen-ya Katana** (p76).

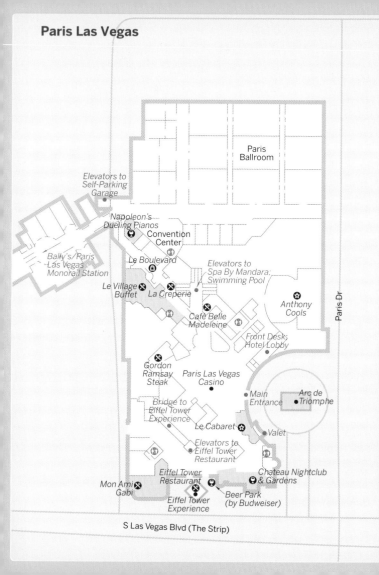

Paris Las Vegas

Paris Ballroom

Elevators to Self-Parking Garage

Napoleon's Dueling Pianos

Convention Center

Bally's/Paris Las Vegas Monorail Station

Le Boulevard

Le Village Buffet

La Creperie

Elevators to Spa By Mandara; Swimming Pool

Anthony Cools

Café Belle Madeleine

Front Desk; Hotel Lobby

Gordon Ramsay Steak

Paris Las Vegas Casino

Bridge to Eiffel Tower Experience

Main Entrance

Arc de Triomphe

Le Cabaret

Valet

Elevators to Eiffel Tower Restaurant

Eiffel Tower Restaurant

Chateau Nightclub & Gardens

Mon Ami Gabi

Beer Park (by Budweiser)

Eiffel Tower Experience

Paris Dr

S Las Vegas Blvd (The Strip)

tropical hardwood, Matisse-styled artworks and silk carpets. Couples can opt for the romantic 'Paris for Lovers' treatment package, delivered with a whirlpool tub made for two. Complimentary fitness center access comes with spa treatments over $50.

Le Cabaret

In a city where entertainment is king, and tickets to a show can cost a small fortune, it's nice to know that some of the good things in life are still free. Just off Paris Las Vegas' casino floor, the intimate **Le Cabaret** (☎702-946-7000; www.caesars.com/paris-las-vegas; Paris Las Vegas; ◷6pm-1am Sun-Thu, to 3am Fri & Sat) hosts a nightly schedule of live jazz where sultry lounge singers will have you almost believing you've stepped into a bar in Saint-Germain.

Chateau Nightclub & Gardens

Hip-hop prevails at this rooftop **venue** (☎702-776-7770; www.chateaunights.com; Paris Las Vegas; ◷10:30pm-4am Wed-Sat) landscaped to look like Parisian gardens. Views over the Strip are divine from tiered outdoor terraces while, back inside, go-go dancers do their thing above a small dancefloor, which can be half empty even on weekends. Sometimes on summer days, the lounge space on the open-air deck doubles as a beer garden.

Napoleon's Dueling Pianos

At this **bar** (☎702-946-7000; www.caesars.com/paris-las-vegas; Paris Las Vegas; ◷5pm-1am), you get whisked off to the never-never land of 19th-century France, with a mosaic floor and overstuffed sofas as luxurious as the menu of 100 types of bubbly, including vintage Dom Pérignon for big spenders. Dueling pianos draw a crowd; there's no cover charge, but expect a two-drink minimum.

Gordon Ramsay Steak

Carnivores, leave Paris behind and stroll through a miniaturized Chunnel into British chef Gordon Ramsay's **steakhouse** (☎877-346-4642; www.gordonramsayrestaurants.com/steak/; Paris Las Vegas; steaks from $50; ◷4:30-10:30pm, to midnight Fri & Sat). Ribboned in red and domed by a jaunty Union Jack, this is one of the top tables in town. Fish, chops and signature beef Wellington round out a menu of Himalayan-salt-room-aged steaks. No reservation? Sit at the bar, instead.

Mon Ami Gabi

Think très charming Champs-Élysées **bistro** (☎702-944-4224; www.monamigabi.com; Paris Las Vegas; mains $12-40; ◷7am-11pm). Breezy patio tables in the shadow of the Eiffel Tower are *parfait* for alfresco dining and watching the Fountains of Bellagio. Though spotty service is far from *magnifique,* it's got classic steak frites and mussels, crepes, quiches and salads, plus a respectable wine list and a special gluten-free menu. Reservations recommended for indoor seating; the patio is first-come, first-served.

Top Experience 📷
Ride a Gondola at Venetian & Palazzo

Inspired by the splendor of Italy's most romantic city, the Venetian (opened in 1999) boasts reproductions of Venetian landmarks. Its grandiose sequel resort, the adjacent Palazzo, threw open its doors to a sophisticated crowd in 2008. You can walk from Vegas' Venice to its offshore island in just a few minutes, but gondoliers are available to complete the experience.

◎ MAP P70, C4 & D4

☏ 702-414-1000

www.venetian.com

3355 S Las Vegas Blvd

⊘ 24hr

🅿

🚌 Deuce

Slice of Italy

Even if you've had the good fortune to stroll the cobblestones and navigate the romantic canals of the world-famous Italian port city, you won't want to miss the Vegas version: in a city filled with spectacles, the Venetian is one of the most magnificent. Graceful bridges, flowing canals and vibrant piazzas faithfully imitate the Venetian spirit.

Architecture

In the ongoing contest for Vegas' best copycat architecture, the Venetian wins the prize for elegant design, just edging ahead of Bellagio, its Italianate rival down the Strip. View the stunning exterior while approaching it over a pedestrian skybridge. Notice the scaled-down replicas of the **Palazzo Ducale**, the towering **Campanile** (bell tower), the mini **Rialto Bridge** (anachronistically equipped with escalators) and a crowded cobblestone **piazza** where tourists gaze down at couples canoodling in gondolas steered by striped-shirted boatiers. Inside the Grand Canal Shoppes (p63), color-fully dressed minstrels and operatic sopranos stroll past patrons sipping wine at faux-outdoor cafes in a miniaturized **Piazza San Marco**.

Gondola Ride

If you can't make it to Venice to experience the real thing, a **gondola ride** (🖉702-414-4300; www.venetian.com/resort/attractions/gondola-rides. html; 3355 S Las Vegas Blvd, Venetian; shared ride per person $29, private 2-passenger ride $116; ⏲indoor rides 10am-11pm Sun-Thu, to midnight Fri & Sat, outdoor rides 11am-9:45pm, weather permitting; 🚻; 🚌Deuce) in Vegas is a touristy activity that nonetheless holds allure for visitors from all over the world. Choose between a moonlit out-door cruise in the resort's miniature lake facing the Strip or float through winding indoor canals past shoppers and diners. Buy tickets inside the Grand Canal Shoppes at the Venetian.

★ **Top Tips**

○ Rooms at Palazzo and Venetian are similar in size, design and price, but the Palazzo is almost a decade younger than its older sister, the Venetian.

○ The gaming floors, Grand Canal Shop-pes and hotel wings of the Palazzo and Venetian are all joined by indoor and outdoor walkways, but taking a gondola ride is a fun (albeit expensive) way to get an overview of Vegas' little slice of Italy.

✕ **Take a Break**

For a happening vibe and the fusion of Latin and Japa-nese cuisine, pop into **Sushisamba** (🖉702-607-0700; www.sushisamba.com; Grand Canal Shoppes at the Palazzo; shared plates from $11, mains from $22; ⏲11:30am-1am, to 2am Fri & Sat).

If alcohol is on your mind, you can't go past the ineffably stylish and recently renovated **Dorsey** (🖉702-414-1945; www. venetian.com; Venetian; ⏲2pm-4am).

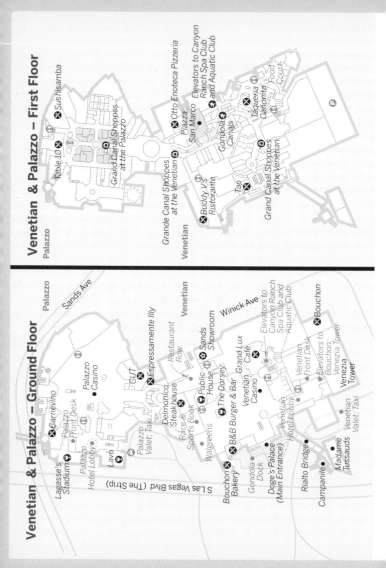

Venetian & Palazzo – First Floor

Palazzo

- ✕ Sushisamba
- ✕ Table 10
- 🛍 Grand Canal Shoppes at the Palazzo
- ✕ Otto Enoteca Pizzeria
- ✕ Elevators to Canyon Ranch Spa Club and Aquatic Club
- Piazza San Marco
- 🛍 Grande Canal Shoppes at the Venetian
- 🚤 Gondola Canals
- ✕ Taqueria Canonita
- 🍴 Food Court
- ✕ Buddy V's Ristorante
- Tao
- 🛍 Grand Canal Shoppes at the Venetian

Venetian

- P

Venetian & Palazzo – Ground Floor

Palazzo

Sands Ave

- ✕ Carnevino
- Palazzo Front Desk
- Palazzo Casino
- ✕ Espressamente Illy
- Restaurant Row

Venetian

Winick Ave

- ✕ Lagasse's Stadium
- 🏨 Palazzo Hotel Lobby
- ✕ CUT
- ✕ Delmonica Steakhouse
- Race & Sports Book
- Palazzo Valet: Taxi
- ✕ Lavo
- 💊 Walgreens
- 🍴 Public House
- 🎭 The Dorsey
- ✕ Grand-Lux Café
- 🎭 Sands Showroom
- Elevators to Canyon Ranch Spa Club and Aquatic Club
- ✕ Bouchon
- Venetian Front Desk
- Elevators to Bouchon; Venezia Tower
- Venetian Casino
- ✕ B&B Burger & Bar
- ✕ S Bouchon Bakery
- Gondola Dock
- 🏨 Venetian Hotel Lobby
- Venezia Tower
- Venetian Valet: Taxi
- Doge's Palace (Main Entrance)
- Rialto Bridge
- Madame Tussauds
- Campanile

S Las Vegas Blvd (The Strip)

Grand Canal Shoppes

Don't be surprised if you come across Hollywood celebrities wandering about the high-design **Grand Canal Shoppes at the Palazzo** (☑702-414-4525; www.grandcanalshoppes.com; 3377 S Las Vegas Blvd, Palazzo; ◷10am-midnight), anchored by the three-story Barneys New York. It's joined to the **Grand Canal Shoppes at the Venetian** (☑702-414-4525; www.grandcanalshoppes.com; 3377 S Las Vegas Blvd, Venetian; ◷10am-11pm Sun-Thu, to midnight Fri & Sat), where wandering painted minstrels, jugglers and laughable living statues perform in Piazza San Marco as gondolas drift by and mezzo-sopranos serenade shoppers. In this airy Italianate mall adorned with frescoes and cobblestone walkways, you'll find an additional 85 luxury boutiques.

Canyon Ranch SpaClub

The modern **Canyon Ranch SpaClub** (☑877-220-2688; www.canyonranch.com/las-vegas; 3355 S Las Vegas Blvd #1159, Grand Canal Shoppes; ◷spa 6am-8pm, salon 9am-7pm), a health-minded spa from Arizona, couldn't feel further from the alleys and canals of Venice, but, nonetheless, here it is. With a focus on well-being and offering more than 100 spa and salon services and fitness activities, it specializes in massage and couples' side-by-side therapies.

On the spa's hydrotherapy circuit, you can move lazily from a herbal laconium to the salt grotto to a meditative wave room. The spa cafe serves light cuisine and fresh fruit smoothies.

Palazzo: Refined Luxury

The sophisticated **Palazzo** lacks a theme, following the Strip's trend toward ever more refined luxury. Forget fun-loving circus acts and exploding volcanoes: the Palazzo is a luxe casino resort best known for its haute cuisine, cool pool club and high-end shopping. Enormous suites come with sunken living rooms and Roman tubs, while Prestige Suites enjoy VIP check-in with complimentary champagne.

Bouchon

Napa Valley wunderkind Thomas Keller's rendition of a Lyonnaise bistro, **Bouchon** (☑702-414-6200; www.thomaskeller.com/bouchonlasvegas; Venetian; mains breakfast & brunch $15-27, dinner $30-60; ◷7am-1pm & 5-10pm Mon-Thu, 7am-2pm & 5-10:30pm Fri-Sun; P ⍝) features a seasonal menu of French classics. The poolside setting complements the oyster bar (open 3pm to 10pm daily) and an extensive raw seafood selection. Decadent breakfasts and brunches, imported cheeses, caviar, foie gras and a superb French and Californian wine list all make appearances. Reservations recommended.

Top Experience 📷

Explore the Exclusive Wynn & Encore

Instead of featuring an exploding volcano or an Eiffel Tower to lure people, casino impresario Steve Wynn's curvaceous, copper-toned twins Wynn (opened in 2005) and Encore (2008) are all about exclusivity. Elements of the casino mogul's former projects peek through: Wynn sports the style of Bellagio but is more vibrant, while Encore feels like a slice of the French Riviera.

◉ MAP P70, D4

📞 702-770-7000

www.wynnlasvegas.com

3131 S Las Vegas Blvd

🕐 24hr

🅿

Wynn

Steve Wynn's signature casino hotel (literally – his name is written in script across the top of the Wynn) exudes secrecy: the entrance is obscured from the Strip by an artificial mountain of greenery, which rises seven stories tall in places. Inside, the resort comes alive with vibrant colors, inlaid flower mosaics, natural-light windows, lush foliage and tumbling waterfalls.

Encore

Wynn's penmanship also labels the adjacent Encore resort, where jeweled peacocks grace the elegant baccarat room and high rollers throw back martinis in cushy casino bars. Sunning yourself at fashionable **Encore Beach Club** (p85) on blazing hot summer days, you might feel like you're an extra in a hip-hop superstar's music video. Back inside the resort, glam **XS** (p84) and Surrender nightclubs host world-renowned DJs and musicians. The extravagant **Spa at Encore** (p67) is the Strip's best for beautifying or, after a big night, detoxifying.

Le Rêve the Dream

Created by ex–Cirque du Soleil director Franco Dragone, the dreamy, fanciful and occasionally nightmarish series of vignettes that make up **Le Rêve the Dream** (☎702-770-9966; http://boxoffice.wynnlasvegas.com; 3131 S Las Vegas Blvd, Wynn; tickets $127-175; ⏰shows 7pm & 9:30pm Fri-Tue; ♿; 🚌Deuce) cost Steve Wynn many millions – and made him more. Underwater acrobatic feats by scuba-certified performers are the centerpiece of this intimate 'aqua-in-the-round' theater, which holds a 1-million-gallon swimming pool. Critics call it a less-inspiring version of Cirque's O, while devoted fans find the romantic underwater tango, thrilling high dives and visually spectacular adventures to be superior. The cheapest seats are in the 'splash zone,' while VIP packages come with champagne and chocolate-covered strawberries.

★ Top Tips

○ As exclusive as Wynn and Encore are, and as stylish as they appear to be, they're both still casinos filled with gaming tables, restaurants and boutiques designed to take your money. Don't be shy: even if you're not a hotel guest, your presence is desired.

○ While the 'twins' look the same from the outside, each has a very different vibe. Of Vegas' return high rollers, Wynn has its staunch supporters, while newer Encore seems to attract a slightly younger, though equally cashed-up crowd, never more evident than at its drool-worthy Beach Club.

✗ Take a Break

Pop into recently refurbished **Parasol Up & Parasol Down** (p67) to rest your legs and sip on classy cocktails.

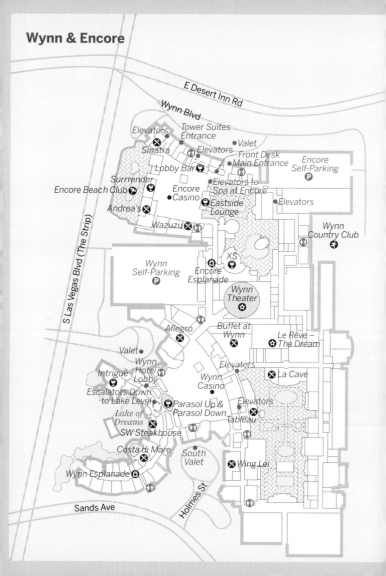

Wynn & Encore

E Desert Inn Rd

Wynn Blvd

Elevators
Tower Suites Entrance
Sinatra
Elevators
• Valet
Lobby Bar
Front Desk
Main Entrance
Encore Self-Parking

Surrrender
Encore Beach Club
Encore Casino
Elevators to Spa at Encore
Eastside Lounge
Elevators

Andrea's
Wazuzu
Wynn Country Club

Wynn Self-Parking
Encore Esplanade
XS

Wynn Theater

Allegro
Buffet at Wynn
Le Rêve – The Dream

Valet •
Wynn Hotel Lobby
Intrigue
Wynn Casino
Elevators
La Cave

Escalators Down to Lake Level
Lake of Dreams
Parasol Up & Parasol Down
Elevators
Tableau

SW Steakhouse
Costa di Mare
South Valet
Wing Lei

Wynn Esplanade

Sands Ave

Holmes St

S Las Vegas Blvd (The Strip)

Intrigue Nightclub

Since its much anticipated opening in spring 2017, Wynn's state-of-the-art nightclub, Intrigue, has been turning heads the length of the Strip with its 14,000ft of after-dark dreams come true: think Studio 54 meets the new millennium. It's chic, sleek and if you don't dress to dazzle you won't even get close to the queue.

Parasol Up & Parasol Down

Stepping into the whimsical jewel-hued **Parasol Up** (📞702-770-3392; www.wynnlasvegas.com; Wynn; ⏰11am-3am Sun-Thu, to 4am Fri & Sat, Parasol Down 11am-2am; 🚌Deuce) feels something like walking into a glamorous version of *Alice in Wonderland*, complete with bright, almost psychedelic flowers. Cozy up on a plush ruby-red loveseat and gaze out at the glassy Lake of Dreams. Down the fairy-tale-like curved escalator, **Parasol Down's** seasonal outdoor patio is the perfect spot for cucumber and ginger-infused martinis.

Costa di Mare

Even in Vegas it doesn't get much posher than **Costa di Mare** (📞702-770-3305; www.wynnlasvegas.com; Wynn; mains $41-62; ⏰5:30-10pm; 🅿❄🍷), where you can book a private cabana beside Wynn's Lake of Dreams and dine on fresh Mediterranean blue rock lobster under a fluttering white canopy. The upscale Italian-style seafood restaurant has a short, highly specialized menu – the whole fish served are indigenous to Italy, and simply prepared. Reservations essential.

Spa at Encore

Newer than the spa at Wynn, Encore's luxurious **spa** (📞702-770-3900; www.wynnlasvegas.com/experiences/spas/encore-spa; Encore; spa day pass guest/nonguest $40/75; ⏰7am-8pm) is splurge-worthy. Stroll down exotic, tranquil passageways lined with flickering Middle Eastern lamps and golden Buddha statues, then sink into hot or cold plunge pools under glowing Swarovski crystal chandeliers, or recline on a heated chaise longue before trying a Thai oil fusion massage or the Moroccan mud wrap. The spa and fitness center entry fee is waived with a treatment of $75 or more.

SW Steakhouse

Bearing Steve Wynn's own initials, **SW Steakhouse** (📞702-770-3325; www.wynnlasvegas.com; Wynn; steaks from $65; ⏰5:30-10pm; ❄) is not just any casino steakhouse: it's perched on the shore of the petite Lake of Dreams. A well-executed classic steakhouse menu hits all the right notes, from oysters on the half shell to chili-rubbed rib-eye steak and black-truffle creamed corn. Reservations are essential, especially for the coveted tables on the open-air terrace.

Walking Tour 🥾

Stroll the Center Strip

The Strip is vast and vibrant, stretching for miles, but some of the most exciting highlights and classic casinos conveniently flank a 1-mile section in the center. You'll hopscotch around Europe with stops in Paris, Venice, Lago di Como and ancient Rome, then get whisked on a side trip to tropical Polynesia. Dancing fountains, belching volcanoes, crooning gondoliers and a half-scale Eiffel Tower are all experiences likely to linger in your memory.

Walk Facts

Start Paris Las Vegas

End Palazzo

Length 1.1 miles; two to four hours

❶ Paris Las Vegas

From the monorail station at the back of Bally's, sashay your way into **Paris Las Vegas** (p56) via the cobblestone shopping arcade Le Boulevard, soaking up *l'atmosphère* and stopping for croissants or crepes. Take a romantic ride up the **Eiffel Tower Experience** (p57) where you can view the **Fountains of Bellagio** (p39) from on high.

❷ Bellagio

Stay in a European mood by sauntering north to Flamingo Rd, then crossing Las Vegas Blvd on a skybridge to **Bellagio** (p38). Inside, admire glass flower sculptures and seasonal floral displays in the conservatory and designer fashions in the glamorous store windows of the Via Bellagio shopping promenade.

❸ Caesars Palace

Take the skybridge across Flamingo Rd and wander down to the plaza outside **Caesars Palace** (p73), where boozy lemonade is dispensed from the Spanish Steps. Inside this fantasia of classical antiquity, watch cocktail waiters dressed in togas parade underneath faux-frescoed ceilings. Meander through the vast **Forum Shops** (p89), then, exiting the mall by the grand spiral staircase, amble north along the Strip toward the tropical paradise of the Mirage.

❹ Mirage

Pause outside the **Mirage** (p75) to watch the faux volcano explode, then step inside the tropically scented hotel lobby to view the 20,000-gallon aquarium and the casino's domed rainforest atrium. If the tropics aren't your thing, channel 1960s London at Cirque du Soleil's show **Beatles LOVE** (p86) and the adjacent Revolution Lounge.

❺ Venetian

Wind down your walk on a graceful note by crossing the Strip toward the elegant **Venetian** (p126), with its flowing canals and mock-marble bridges. Treat yourself to a **gondola ride** (p61) with a singing gondolier or glide on your own feet through the **Grand Canal Shoppes** (p63), then indulge in a well-deserved scoop of gelato at busy St Mark's Sq.

❻ Palazzo

Keep winding your way through the Grand Canal Shoppes into the **Palazzo** (p63), where a photo op in front of the indoor waterfall proves irresistible for many. To get back to where you started, catch the monorail at nearby Harrah's.

The Strip

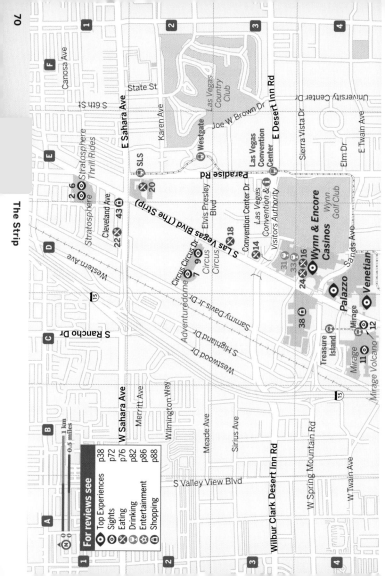

F
Canosa Ave
State St
S 6th St
E Sahara Ave
Karen Ave
Las Vegas Country Club
Joe W Brown Dr

E
Stratosphere Thrill Rides
2 6
Cleveland Ave
22 🍽️ 43 🍽️
Las Vegas Convention Center
E Desert Inn Rd
SLS 🚇
20 🍽️
Las Vegas Convention Center Dr
Paradise Rd
Elvis Presley Blvd
18 🍽️
Convention Center Dr
Las Vegas Convention & Visitors Authority ℹ️
14 🍽️
Sierra Vista Dr
Elm Dr
E Twain Ave
University Center Dr
Westgate

D
Stratosphere
Western Ave
S Las Vegas Blvd (The Strip)
Circus Circus Dr
Circus Circus
7 9
Adventuredome
Sammy Davis Jr Dr
S Highland Dr
Wynn & Encore Casinos
Wynn Golf Club
31
33
24 🍽️ 16 🍽️
38
Sands Ave
Palazzo
Venetian

C
S Rancho Dr
Westwood Dr
Wilmington Way
Meade Ave
Sirius Ave
S Valley View Blvd
Treasure Island
Mirage
Mirage Volcano
11
12

B
W Sahara Ave
Merritt Ave
Wilbur Clark Desert Inn Rd
W Spring Mountain Rd
W Twain Ave

A
1 km
0.5 miles

For reviews see
◎ Top Experiences p38
◉ Sights p72
✗ Eating p76
🍷 Drinking p82
🎭 Entertainment p86
🛍️ Shopping p88

1
2
3
4

Getting into Nightclubs

Before braving a nightclub's velvet rope and shelling out big bucks for the cover charge, look for the club's own promoters, usually standing on the casino floor of the corresponding hotel or resort – they're giving out passes for expedited entry and free drinks, especially to well-dressed women. Alternatively, book ahead with a club promoter such as Chris Hornak of **Free Vegas Club Passes** (www.freevegasclubpasses.com).

Sights

LINQ Casino
CASINO

1 ◉ MAP P70, C5

With a fresh, young and funky vibe, one of Vegas' newest casinos benefits from also being one of its smallest with just over 60 tables and around 750 slot machines. There's an airy, spacious feel to the place, tables feature high-backed, ruby-red, patent-vinyl chairs, and when you need to escape, the fun and frivolity of LINQ Promenade (p50) are just outside the door. (📞800-634-6441; www.caesars.com/linq; 3535 S Las Vegas Blvd; ⏱24hr; P)

Stratosphere
CASINO

2 ◉ MAP P70, E1

Vegas has many buildings more than 20 stories tall, but only Stratosphere exceeds 100 and features the nation's highest thrill rides. Atop the 1149ft-high tapered tripod tower, vertiginous indoor and outdoor viewing decks afford Vegas' best 360-degree panoramas. There you'll also find Top of the World (p80), a revolving restaurant, (📞702-380-7777; www.stratospherehotel.com; 2000 S Las Vegas Blvd; tower adult/child $20/10, all-day pass incl unlimited thrill rides $40; ⏱casino 24hr, tower & thrill rides 10am-1am Sun-Thu, to 2am Fri & Sat, weather permitting; P♿)

MGM Grand
CASINO

3 ◉ MAP P70, C7

Owned by the eponymous Hollywood studio, the Grand liberally borrows Hollywood themes. Flashing LED screens and computerized fountains add extra theatrics to the 100,000lb, 45ft-tall bronze lion statue at the casino's entrance. Inside the labyrinthine casino bedecked with giant screens, you can get table-side massages or take free Texas hold'em lessons in the poker room. Top billing attractions include Hakkasan (p82) nightclub, one-time center of the electronic dance-music universe, Cirque du Soleil's martial-arts-inspired Kà (📞702-531-3826; www.cirquedusoleil.com/ka; MGM Grand; adult $69-250; ⏱7pm & 9:30pm Sat-Wed; ♿) and the massive **MGM Grand Garden Arena** (📞877-880-0880; www.mgmgrand.com; MGM Grand; ticket prices vary; ⏱box office 9am-8:30pm). (📞877-880-0880; www.mgmgrand.com; 3799 S Las Vegas Blvd; ⏱24hr; P♿)

Caesars Palace

CASINO

4 MAP P70, C5

Caesars Palace claims that more players have won million-dollar slots than anywhere in the world, but its claims to fame are far more numerous than that. Entertainment heavyweights perform at the massive Colosseum (p87) theater, fashionistas saunter around The Forum Shops (p89), while Caesars' hotel guests quaff cocktails in the Garden of the Gods Pool Oasis (p83) is one of the best places to get off your face this side of Ibiza. (866-227-5938; www.caesars.com/caesars-palace; 3570 S Las Vegas Blvd; 24hr; P; Deuce)

Qua Baths & Spa

SPA

5 MAP P70, C5

Qua evokes the ancient Roman rituals of indulgent bathing. Try a signature 'bath liqueur,' a personalized potion of herbs and oils poured into your own private tub. The women's side includes a tea lounge, a herbal steam room and an Arctic ice room where artificial snow falls. On the men's side, there's a barber spa and big-screen sports TVs. (866-782-0655; www.caesars.com/caesars-palace; Caesars Palace; fitness center day pass $25, incl spa facilities $50; 6am-8pm)

Stratosphere Thrill Rides

AMUSEMENT PARK

6 MAP P70, E1

The world's highest thrill rides await, a whopping 110 stories above

MGM Grand

the Strip. Big Shot straps riders into completely exposed seats that zip up the tower's pinnacle, while Insanity spins riders out over the tower's edge. X-Scream leaves you hanging 27ft over the edge, 866ft above ground. For a real adrenaline rush, save your dough for **SkyJump** (☏702-380-7777; www.skyjumplasvegas.com; Stratosphere; per jump $130; ⏱10am-1am Sun-Thu, to 2am Fri & Sat). (☏702-380-7777; www.stratospherehotel.com/ThrillRides; Stratosphere; elevator adult $20, incl 3 thrill rides $35, all-day pass $40; ⏱10am-1am Sun-Thu, to 2am Fri & Sat; 🖳Sahara)

Adventuredome AMUSEMENT PARK

7 ◉ MAP P70, D2

Circus Circus' indoor amusement park is packed with thrills: must-rides include the double-loop,

Sky Jump at the Stratosphere (p72)

ZRZVZNER/SHUTTERSTOCK ©

double-corkscrew Canyon Blaster and the El Loco that packs a whopping -1.5 Gs of vertical acceleration. Older kids get a rock-climbing wall, bungee-jumping area, mini golf and 4D special-effect 'ridefilms.' Clowns perform free shows throughout the day. (☏702-794-3939; www.adventuredome.com; Circus Circus; day pass over/under 48in tall $34/20; ⏱10am-midnight, varies seasonally; 🚼)

Welcome to Las Vegas Sign LANDMARK

8 ◉ MAP P70, C8

In a city famous for neon signs, one reigns supreme: the 'Welcome to Fabulous Las Vegas Nevada' sign, facing north and straddling Las Vegas Blvd just south of Mandalay Bay (p42), the unofficial start of the Strip. Designed by Betty Willis in the 'Fabulous Fifties,' this is a classic photo op and a reminder of Vegas' past. Only southbound traffic can enter the parking lot/ (5200 S Las Vegas Blvd; admission free; ⏱24hr; 🚼)

Circus Circus LANDMARK

9 ◉ MAP P70, D2

If you belong to that special bunch of people who are terrified by clowns, do not under any circumstances venture near this somewhat bedraggled part of the north Strip: if the enormous clown sign isn't impossible to handle, you'll lose it at the clown-shaped marquee (there are real-life clowns inside). Although this ole circus with its bigtop casino is as cheesy as it looks, it's also lots of fun, especially if you have kids.

(📞702-734-0410; www.circuscircus.com; 2880 S Las Vegas Blvd; admission free; ⏲24hr; 👫 P)

Luxor
CASINO

10 ◎ MAP P70, C7

Named after Egypt's ancient city, the Luxor once had the biggest wow factor on the south Strip. While the theme easily could have produced a pyramid of gaudiness, instead it resulted in a relatively refined shrine to Egyptian art and antiquities. Luxor's casino floor is slightly frantic and confusing layout, with a few thousand slots, more than 100 gaming tables, and a race and sports book. (📞702-262-4000; www.luxor.com; 3900 S Las Vegas Blvd; ⏲24hr; P)

Mirage
CASINO

11 ◎ MAP P70, C4

Having partially shaken off its tropical theme, the Mirage retains its huge rain forest atrium of lush, tropical foliage and has updated the 20,000-gallon saltwater aquarium in the lobby. The casino floor features a sports book, huge Center Bar, more than 100 tables and over 2000 slots, and a poker room offering daily tournaments and complimentary lessons. (📞702-791-7111; www.mirage.com; 3400 S Las Vegas Blvd; ⏲24hr; P)

Mirage Volcano
LANDMARK

12 ◎ MAP P70, C4

When the Mirage's trademark artificial volcano erupts with a roar out of

Public Oasis

For some reason in such a sunshine-filled place, it took 60 years for an outdoor park to be built on the Las Vegas Strip. The new-in-2016 **Park** (📞702-693-7275; www.theparkvegas.com/en.html; 3782 S Las Vegas Blvd; 👫) is a public place with plenty of visual appeal; waterworks and fountains line tree-shaded pathways festooned with restaurants, such as the eatery Bruxie where Belgian waffles are united with fried chicken. Rare for the Strip, it's a place that's suitable for children as well as adults.

a 3-acre lagoon, it inevitably brings traffic on the Strip to a screeching halt. Look for wisps of smoke escaping from the top, signaling that the fiery Polynesian-style inferno, with music by a Grateful Dead drummer and an Indian tabla musician, is about to begin. (📞702-791-7111; www.mirage.com; Mirage; admission free; ⏲shows 8pm, 9pm & 10pm daily)

Flamingo Wildlife Habitat
GARDENS

13 ◎ MAP P70, C5

Slip away from the madness inside the **Flamingo's** (📞702-733-3111; www.caesars.com/flamingo-las-vegas; 3555 S Las Vegas Blvd; ⏲24hr; P) wildlife habitat, out back behind the casino. Over a dozen acres of pools, gardens, waterfalls and waterways are filled with swans, exotic birds and ornamental koi (carp). Here, Chilean flamingos and African penguins wander around, and palm trees and jungle plants flourish in the middle of the desert. (☏702-733-3349; www.caesars.com/flamingo-las-vegas; Flamingo; admission free; ☉dawn-dusk, pelican feedings 8:30am & 2pm; ℗🛗)

Eating

Tacos El Gordo MEXICAN $

14 ✖ MAP P70, D3

This Tijuana–style taco shop from SoCal is just the ticket when it's way late, you've got almost no money left and you're desperately craving *carne asada* (beef) or *adobada* (chili-marinated pork) tacos in hot, handmade tortillas. (☏702-331-1160; www.tacoselgordobc.com; 3041 S Las Vegas Blvd; dishes $2.60-5; ☉10am-2am, to 4am Fri & Sat; ℗🛗; 🚌Deuce)

Ramen-ya Katana RAMEN $

15 ✖ MAP P70, C5

Granted, purists who follow the Japanese religion of ramen might get picky, but we won't. In a sea of complicated, overpriced and prohibitive dining, Katana offers humble bowls of hot broth swimming with hearty noodles at *almost* normal prices, on the center Strip. In true fusion fashion, they've even thrown sushi burritos on the menu. Winning! (☏702-586-6889; www.ramen-katanaya.com; 3615 S Las Vegas

Blvd, Grand Bazaar Shops; meals $9-14; ☉10am-11pm; ❄)

La Cave MEDITERRANEAN $$

16 ✖ MAP P70, D4

Flavorful seasonal tapas, brick-oven-fired flatbreads and Mediter-ranean-inspired plates, all meant for sharing, are the ticket at this good-value, laid-back hideaway. With romantic candlelight, Spanish-style archways and a pretty pool-view patio, La Cave is a secluded spot for a dinner date or a few glasses of tempranillo with an artisanal cheese or charcuterie board. (☏702-770-7375; www.wynnlasvegas.com; Wynn; mains from $17; ☉11:30am-9:30pm Sun-Thu, to 10pm Fri & Sat; ℗🍸)

Guy Fieri's Vegas Kitchen & Bar AMERICAN $$

Diners, Drive-ins and Dives celebrity chef Guy Fieri has opened his first restaurant on the Strip at LINQ Casino (see 1 ◉ Map p70, C5), dishing out an eclectic menu of his own design, inspired by so many years journeying America's back roads for the best down-home cooking. (☏702-794-3139; www.caesars.com/linq; LINQ Casino; mains $19-35; ☉9am-midnight)

Grand Wok CHINESE $$

Come to Grand Wok (see 3 ◉ Map p70, C6), in business for over 25 years serving some of the best pan-Asian dishes you'll find this side of the Far East. Try the garlic shrimp fried rice with dried scallops. Sensational. (☏702-891-7879; www.mgmgrand.com/en/restaurants.html;

MGM Grand; mains $12-28; 🕙11am-10pm Sun-Thu, to 11pm Fri & Sat)

Burger Bar

AMERICAN $$

17 ✕ MAP P70, C8

Since when can a hamburger be worth $65? When it's built with Kobe beef, sautéed foie gras and truffle sauce: it's the Rossini burger, the signature sandwich of chef Hubert Keller. Most menu options are more down-to-earth – diners select their own gourmet burger toppings and pair them with skinny fries and a liquor-spiked milkshake or beer float. (📞702-632-9364; http://burgerbarlv.com; Shoppes at Mandalay Place; burgers $20; 🕙11am-11pm Sun-Thu, to midnight Fri & Sat; P ❄ 👪)

Searsucker Las Vegas

GASTROPUB $$$

Searsucker is a heavy hitter serving punchy small plates and killer cocktails in casual digs with a cowboy twang on Caesars' (see 4 👁 Map p70, C5) gaming floor. There's a daily happy hour and a modern American menu that has something for everyone. (📞702-866-1800; www.searsucker.com/las-vegas; Caesars Palace; mains from $31; 🕙5-11pm Sun, Mon, Wed & Thu, to midnight Tue, Fri & Sat)

Peppermill

DINER $$

18 ✕ MAP P70, D3

Slide into a crescent-shaped booth at this retro casino coffee shop and revel in the old-school Vegas atmosphere. You can eavesdrop on

Tacos El Gordo

MARK READ/LONELY PLANET ©

Joël Rubochon restaurant

Nevada cowboys and downtown politicos digging into a gigantic late-night bite or early breakfast. For tropical tiki drinks, step into a sexy booth at Peppermill's Fireside Lounge (p85). (☏702-735-4177; www.peppermilllasvegas.com; 2985 S Las Vegas Blvd; mains $13-31; ⊙24hr)

China Poblano   FUSION $$

Noodles and tacos, together? An eye-catching fusion eatery (see 39 🔒 Map p70, C6) from chef José Andrés mixes two unlikely cuisines – Chinese and Mexican – in a lively, hipster-friendly space where the glow of neon signs brightens darkened booths and barstools. Inspired street-food riffs include duck-tongue tacos with lychee and red-chili-braised pork buns. (☏702-698-7900; www.chinapoblano.com; Cosmopolitan; shared plates $13-20;

⊙11:30am-11pm Sun-Thu, to 11:30pm Fri & Sat; P❄️🖋️)

Cravings   BUFFET $$

Not the best, but far from the worst of the Strip's buffets, Cravings (see 11 ◉ Map p70, C4), will probably leave you feeling you got your money's worth, with 11 live-action cooking stations, Goose Island IPA on tap and life-changing chocolate croissant bread pudding for dessert. Rather eat in your room? Ask about the takeout special ($16) that lets you fill up a to-go box. (☏702-791-7111; www.mirage.com; Mirage; per adult $19-33, per child 5-10yr $13-23; ⊙7am-9pm Mon-Fri, from 8am Sat & Sun; P❄️🖋️👫)

Morimoto   FUSION $$$

Iron Chef Masaharu Morimoto's latest Vegas incarnation is in his eponymous showcase restaurant (see 3 ◉ Map p70, C6), which pays homage to his Japanese roots and the cuisine of this city that has propelled him to legend status around the world. Dining here is an experience in every possible way and, we think, worth every penny. (☏702-891-3001; www.mgmgrand.com; MGM Grand; mains $24-75; ⊙5-10pm)

Joël Robuchon   FRENCH $$$

Joel Robuchon, the acclaimed 'Chef of the Century', leads the pack in the French culinary invasion of the Strip. His eponymous art deco-inspired dining room (see 3 ◉ Map p70, C6), done up in leather and purple velvet, exudes the sophistication of a dinner party at a 1930s Paris mansion. Complex seasonal tasting menus promise the meal of a lifetime – and they often deliver. (☎702-891-7925; www.mgmgrand.com; 3799 S Las Vegas Blvd, MGM Grand; tasting menus $130-445; ⏱5:30-10pm; P; 🚊Deuce)

Restaurant Guy Savoy
FRENCH $$$

With Strip-view picture windows, this exclusive dining room (see 4 ◉ Map p70, C5) is the only US restaurant by three-star Michelin chef Guy Savoy. Both the culinary concepts and the prices reach heavenly heights. If you just want a small taste, perhaps of artichoke black-truffle soup or crispy-skinned sea bass, sit in the Cognac Lounge for drinks and nibbles. Dinner reservations are essential. (☎702-731-7286; www.caesars.com/caesars-palace; Caesars Palace; mains $80-110, tasting menus $120-350; ⏱5:30-9:30pm Wed-Sun)

Border Grill
MEXICAN $$$

19 ❌ MAP P70, C8

With colorful murals and views over Mandalay Bay Beach (p43), this festive eatery dishes up modern Mexican fare designed by chefs from Bravo's *Top Chef Masters* and the Food Network's *Too Hot Tamales*. Come for the weekend brunch of unlimited Latin-inspired tapas ($38) and bottomless mimosas (extra $15). Border Grill uses only hormone-free meat and sustainably caught seafood. Reservations are helpful. (☎702-632-7403; www.bordergrill.com; Mandalay Bay; mains $17-36; ⏱11am-10pm, Mon-Fri, from 10am Sat & Sun; P🖋🚻)

Bazaar Meat
STEAK $$$

20 ❌ MAP P70, E2

Rockstar Spanish chef José Andrés is at the helm of this **SLS** (☎702-761-7000; www.slslasvegas.com; 2535 S Las Vegas Blvd; d from $102; P❄🛜🚻) headline restaurant that offers a twist on the traditional steakhouse, inventively blending disparate flavors and cultures with mouthwatering success. The meaty menu does have some seafood (including a raw bar) for pescatarians, but vegetarians will want to look elsewhere. (☎855-761-7757; www.slslasvegas.com; SLS; mains $45; ⏱5:30-10pm; P❄)

Hash House a Go Go
AMERICAN $$

Fill up on this SoCal import's 'twisted farm food,' (see 1 ◉ Map p70, C5) which has to be seen to be believed. The pancakes are as big as tractor tires, while farm-egg scrambles and housemade hashes could knock over a cow. Meatloaf, pot pies, chicken 'n' biscuits and wild-boar sloppy joes are what's for breakfast, but it's more popular for breakfast and brunch. (☎702-254-4646; www.hashhouseagogo.com; LINQ; mains breakfast & lunch from $11, dinner from $19; ⏱24hr; ❄🚻)

Le Village Buffet

BUFFET $$$

21 ⊗ MAP P70, C5

An incredible array of fruits and cheeses, a toasty range of breads and pastries, and macaroons for dessert make this one of the best-value buffets on the Strip. Distinct cooking stations are themed by France's various regions, with an emphasis on seafood. Breakfasts are excellent, and so are weekend brunches. (☎702-946-7000; www.caesars.com/paris-las-vegas; Paris Las Vegas; buffet $25-40; ⏰7am-10am & 3-10pm, Sun-Thu, to 11pm Fri & Sat; ✍👪)

Bacchanal

BUFFET $$$

As over-the-top as Caesars Palace's (see 4 ◉ Map p70, C5), statuary of Roman deities, this is the Strip's most expansive and expensive buffet. An all-you-can-eat feast of king crab legs, housemade sushi and dim sum, oak-grilled BBQ, baked-to-order soufflés and so much more goes beyond what you could ever possibly taste in one sitting. Windows overlook the Garden of the Gods pools. (☎702-731-7928; www.caesars.com; Caesars Palace; buffet per adult $40-65, child 5-10yr $20-35; ⏰7:30am-10pm, from 8am Sat & Sun; P❄✍👪)

Golden Steer

STEAK $$$

22 ⊗ MAP P70, D1

The Rat Pack, Marilyn Monroe and Elvis all dined at this fabulously retro steakhouse with the steer's head out front. Soak up the vintage Vegas vibes. (☎702-384-4470; www.

goldensteersteakhouselasvegas.com; 308 W Sahara Ave; steaks from $47; ⏰4:30-10:30pm; ✍; 🚌SDX)

Top of the World

AMERICAN $$$

While taking in the cloud-level views at this revolving romantic roost (see 2 ◉ Map p70, E1) perched atop the Stratosphere (p72) tower, smartly dressed diners enjoy impeccable service and satisfying, if overpriced, dishes such as New Zealand rack of lamb with basil mint pistou or swordfish in beurre blanc. Excellent wine list. Reservations essential. (☎702-380-7711; www.topoftheworldlv.com; Stratosphere; mains from $44; ⏰11am-11pm)

Rivea

EUROPEAN $$$

23 ⊗ MAP P70, C8

Atop **Delano** (☎702-632-7888; www.delanolasvegas.com; 3950 S Las Vegas Blvd, Mandalay Bay; r weekday/weekend from $143/369; P❄@🛜🐾👪), Rivea's upscale French-Italian dining from celebrity chef Alain Ducasse, stands on its own, but the real pull here is the classy but casual atmosphere and the incomparable indoor and patio views of the Strip. (☎702-632-9500; https://delanolasvegas.mgmresorts.com; Delano, Mandalay Bay; mains $24-72, tasting menus from $115; ⏰6-10pm, to 10:30pm Fri & Sat)

Buffet at Wynn

BUFFET $$$

24 ⊗ MAP P70, D4

Wynn's (p64) buffet is an upscale version of the average all-you-can-eat feed. A color palette of butter yellow, sea green and dusty rose, with flowers bursting out of vases everywhere, lends some dignity to the gluttony of 15 live-action cooking stations, piles of cracked crab legs and an unlimited dessert bar. (📞702-770-3340; www.wynnlas vegas.com; Wynn; per person $32-60; ⏰7:30am-9:30pm; 🅿️ ❄️ 🖋️ 👪)

Stripsteak

STEAK $$$

25 🍴 MAP P70, C8

Esquire magazine once named chef Michael Mina's butter-poached, bone-in-top loin one of the USA's very best steaks. The chef's minimalist steakhouse knifes into an exceptional menu of all-natural Angus and American Kobe beef, taste-awakening appetizers like ahi tuna and hamachi poppers, and classic side dishes with a twist, from truffle mac 'n' cheese to soy-glazed green beans.

Reservations essential. (📞702-632-7200; www.michaelmina.net; Mandalay Bay; mains from $41; ⏰4-10pm)

Nobu

JAPANESE, FUSION $$$

Iron Chef Nobu Matsuhisa's sequel to his NYC establishment (see 4 ◎ Map p70, C5) is almost as good as the original. The setting is postmodern Zen, with glowing yellow lanterns, private dining 'pods' and sociable *teppanyaki* grill tables. Stick with Nobu's classics such as black cod with miso, South American–influenced *tiradito* (a lighter version of ceviche), spicy edamame and fusion sushi rolls. Reservations essential. (📞702-785-6628; www. noburestaurants.com; Caesars Palace; shared plates $5-60, lunch mains $22-50, dinner tasting menus $90-500; ⏰5-11pm Sun-Thu, to midnight Sat & Sun)

Bacchanal

Wicked Spoon Buffet

🍴

Wicked Spoon (📞877-893-2001; www.cosmopolitanlasvegas.com; Chelsea Tower, 2708 S Las Vegas Blvd, Cosmopolitan; brunch/dinner from $29/42; ⏱8am-9pm Sun-Thu, 8am-10pm Fri & Sat; 🅿❄♿; 🚌Deuce) makes casino buffets seem cool again, with freshly prepared temptations served on individual plates for you to grab and take back to your table. The spread has all the expected meat, sushi, seafood and desserts, but with global upgrades – think roasted bone marrow and a gelato bar. Weekend brunch adds unlimited champagne mimosas or Bloody Marys (surcharge $10).

Spice Market Buffet

BUFFET $$$

26 🍴 MAP P70, C6

Middle Eastern, Asian, Italian and Mexican fare are thrown into the global mix at this jewel of a buffet, a throwback to the original Aladdin resort. Attentive service, above-average desserts and live-action cooking stations justify the often very long waits to be seated. (📞702-785-5555; www.caesars.com/planet-hollywood; Planet Hollywood; buffet adult/child $26/18; ⏱7am-11pm; 🍴♿)

Todd English's Olives

MEDITERRANEAN $$$

27 🍴 MAP P70, C5

East Coast chef Todd English pays homage to the ancient life-giving fruit at this Italian-inflected eatery. Flatbread pizza, housemade pasta and grilled meats get top billing. The chef's table faces a bustling open kitchen, while the patio overlooks Lake Como. With an exceptional wine list and flamboyant desserts, it's always packed – come for lunch but, even then, make reservations first(📞702-693-8181; www.toddenglish.com; Bellagio; mains lunch $17-29. dinner $25-49; ⏱restaurant 11am-2:45pm & 5-10:30pm, bar 3-5pm; 🍴🅿)

Buffet at Bellagio

BUFFET $$$

28 🍴 MAP P70, C5

Bellagio once competed for honors among Vegas' live-action buffets, but lately it has become second-tier. It's most satisfying at breakfast or lunch. The more varied dinnertime spread features seafood and creative dishes from around the world – too bad they don't all taste as good as they look. (📞702-693-8865; http://bellagio.mgmresorts.com; Bellagio; per person $25-44; ⏱7am-10pm; 🅿❄)

Drinking

Hakkasan

CLUB

At this lavish Asian-inspired nightclub (see 3 ⊙ Map p70, C6), international EDM jet-set DJs such as Tiësto and Steve Aoki rule the packed main dance floor bordered by VIP booths and floor-to-ceiling LED screens. More offbeat sounds spin in the intimate Ling Ling Club, with leather sofas and backlit amber glass. (☎702-891-3838; http://hakkasannightclub.com; 3799 S Las Vegas Blvd, MGM Grand; cover women/men from $20/30; ☺10:30pm-4am Thu-Sun; ☐Deuce)

Omnia
CLUB

29 ☺ MAP P70, C5

Hakkasan group's Caesars megaclub exudes a Miami Beach vibe and has residencies by top spinners like Calvin Harris and Martin Garrix. Dance the night away to high-octane Top 40/hip-hop beneath a kinetic chandelier whose eight circles create ever-changing visual effects. (☎702-785-6200; www.omniaclubs.com/las-vegas; 3570 S Las Vegas Blvd, Caesars Palace; cover women/men from $20/30; ☺10:30pm-4am Tue & Thu-Sun; ☐Deuce)

Marquee
CLUB

The Cosmopolitan's (p53) glam nightclub (see 3 🔒 Map p70, C6), cashes in on its multimillion-dollar sound system and a happening dance floor surrounded by towering LED screens displaying light projections that complement EDM tracks hand-picked by famous DJs. From late spring through early fall, Marquee's mega-popular daytime pool club heads outside to a lively party deck overlooking the Strip, with VIP cabanas and bungalows. (☎702-333-9000;

The Strip Drinking

Hakkasan

JEFFREY J COLEMAN/SHUTTERSTOCK ©

XS

www.marqueelasvegas.com; Cosmopolitan; ⏱10:30pm-5am Mon, Fri & Sat)

Jewel
CLUB

30 🚇 MAP P70, C6

Jewel is a luxe dancing den that considers itself 'intimate' despite squeezing as many as 2000 shiny happy people into its sparkling space. Designers have made maximum use of LED technology to fuel the action in the main club. High-rollers can retreat into five themed suites on the mezzanine. (📞702-590-8000; www.jewelnightclub.com; 3730 S Las Vegas Blvd, Aria; female/male from $20/30; ⏱10:30pm-4am Fri, Sat & Mon; 🚌Deuce)

XS
CLUB

31 🚇 MAP P70, D3

A few years in, XS is hitting its stride. Its extravagantly gold-drenched decor and over-the-top design mean you'll be waiting in line for cocktails at a bar towered over by ultra-curvaceous, larger-than-life golden statues of female torsos. Famous electronica DJs make the dance floor writhe, while high rollers opt for VIP bottle service at private poolside cabanas. (📞702-770-0097; www.xslasvegas.com; Encore; cover $20-30; ⏱10:30pm-4am Fri-Sun)

Wet Republic
CLUB

Think of Wet Republic (see 3 ◉ Map p70, C6), the city's biggest 'ultra pool,' as a nightclub brought out into the sunlight. The mostly 20- and 30-something crowd in stylish swimwear show up for EDM tunes spun by megawatt DJs like Calvin Harris, fruity cocktails and bobbing oh-so-coolly around saltwater pools while checking out the bikini-clad scenery. Book ahead for VIP bungalows, daybeds and cabanas. (702-891-3563; www.wetrepublic.com; MGM Grand; cover $20-40; ☺11am-6pm Thu-Mon)

Fireside Lounge

LOUNGE

Don't be blinded by the outlandishly bright neon outside. The Strip's most spellbinding retro hideaway (see 18 ✖ Map p70, E2) awaits at the pint-sized Peppermill (p77) casino. Courting couples adore the sunken firepit, fake tropical foliage and 64oz goblet-sized 'Scorpion' cocktails served by waiters in black evening gowns. (702-735-7635; www.peppermilllasvegas.com; 2985 S Las Vegas Blvd, Peppermill; ☺24hr; ☐Deuce)

Drai's Beachclub & Nightclub

CLUB

32 ☐ MAP P70, C5

Feel ready for an after-hours party scene straight outta Hollywood? Or maybe you just wanna hang out all day poolside, then shake your booty on the petite dance floor while DJ royalty spin hip-hop, mash-ups and electronica? This multi-venue rooftop club has you covered pretty much all day and night. Dress to kill: no sneakers, sandals or baggy clothing. (702-777-3800; www.draisgroup.com/las-vegas/; 3595 S Las Vegas Blvd, Cromwell Las Vegas; nightclub cover women $20-50, men

$30-100; ☺nightclub 10:30pm-4am Fri-Sun, beach club 11am-6pm Fri-Sun, after-hours 2am-10am; ☐Deuce)

Encore Beach Club

CLUB

33 ☐ MAP P70, D3

Soak up sunshine on a larger-than-life 'lilypad,' bob around the pool to DJ-spun tunes, play high-stakes blackjack by the pool or kick back in a private bungalow or cabana with its own hot tub. The club features three tiered pools (one with an island platform for dancing), plus a gaming pavilion and top international DJs. (702-770-7300; www.encorebeachclub.com; Encore; cover $35-55; ☺11am-7pm Fri & Sun, from 10am Sat)

Chandelier Lounge

COCKTAIL BAR

Towering high in the Cosmopolitan (p53), this ethereal cocktail bar (see 3 ☐ Map p70, C6), is inventive yet beautifully simple, with three levels

Cashless Rides

Cashless rideshare services booked through your smartphone (such as Uber and Lyft) are the cheapest, most convenient and most efficient way to get around Vegas. There's a glut of eager drivers trying to outshine each other for your post-ride five-star ratings, picking you up in spotless chariots, and often offering bottled water and tailored playlists in surround sound.

connected by curved staircases, draped with glowing glass beads. The second level is headquarters for experimental concoctions, while the third specializes in floral and fruit infusions. (📞702-698-7979; www.cosmopolitanlasvegas.com; 3708 S Las Vegas Blvd, Cosmopolitan; 🕐24hr; 🚌Deuce)

Tea Lounge LOUNGE

34 🚇 MAP P70, C6

With glittering Strip views from the panoramic windows of the hotel's 23rd-floor 'sky lobby,' this sophisticated lounge serves exotic teas by day and champagne cocktails by night. Make reservations for afternoon tea (from $36, available 1pm to 5pm daily). (📞702-590-8888; www.waldorfastorialasvegas.com; Waldorf Astoria, CityCenter; 🕐lounge

10am-10pm daily, bar noon-2am Fri & Sat, 4pm-1am Sun-Thu; 🎰)

Entertainment

Blue Man Group LIVE PERFORMANCE

Art, music and technology combine with a dash of comedy in one of Vegas' most popular, family-friendly shows (see 10 🔘 Map p70, C7), at Luxor (p75). (📞702-262-4400; www.blueman.com; Luxor; tickets $59-130; 🕐shows at 7pm & 9:30pm; 👪)

Beatles LOVE THEATER

Another smash hit from Cirque du Soleil, *Beatles LOVE* (see 11 🔘 Map p70, C4), started as the brainchild of the late George Harrison. Using *Abbey Road* master tapes, the show psychedelically fuses the musical

Colosseum

legacy of the Beatles with Cirque's high-energy dancers and signature aerial acrobatics. Come early to photograph the trippy, rainbow-colored entryway. (☎702-792-7777; www.cirquedusoleil.com/beatles-love; 3400 S Las Vegas Blvd, Mirage; tickets $60-185; ⏱7pm & 9:30pm Tue-Sat; 🚻; 🚌Deuce)

Criss Angel Mindfreak Live
LIVE PERFORMANCE

Find out why Criss Angel is the most watched magician in history in what is billed as the greatest magic spectacle (see 26 ✖ Map p70, C7), of all time, at Planet Hollywood. (https://crissangel.com/planet-hollywood-mind-freak; Planet Hollywood; tickets from $70; ⏱shows 7pm Wed-Sun)

T-Mobile Arena
CONCERT VENUE

35 ⭐ MAP P70, C7

New in 2016 and costing a cool $375 million, Las Vegas' premier stadium occupies a prime spot on the Strip and boasts 24 private boxes, 54 suites and seating for up to 20,000 people. Las Vegas' professional hockey team slides around here, as do acts like Jennifer Lopez when she's in town. (☎702-692-1600; www.t-mobilearena.com; 3780 S Las Vegas Blvd; ⏱box office noon-6pm)

Park Theater
CONCERT VENUE

36 ⭐ MAP P70, C7

Stage one of Monte Carlo's rebranding as **Park MGM** (https://parkmgm.mgmresorts.com; 3770 S Las Vegas Blvd; r from $109; 🅿❄🛜♿),

Last-Minute Tickets

Tix 4 Tonight (☎877-849-4868; www.tix4tonight.com; 3200 S Las Vegas Blvd, Fashion Show Mall; ⏱10am-8pm) offers half-price tickets for a limited lineup of same-day shows and small discounts on 'always sold-out' shows. It's located outside Neiman Marcus department store. Check the website for other locations around the Strip.

this state-of-the-art, 5000-plus-seat concert venue plays host to acts such as Lady Gaga and Janet Jackson. (☎844-600-7275; www.mgmresorts.com; 3770 S Las Vegas Blvd; ticket prices vary; ⏱box office 9am-6pm)

Colosseum
LIVE PERFORMANCE

A high-tech version of ancient Rome's famous arena (but without the gladiator fights), this 4300-seat venue (see 4 ◉ Map p70, C5) has state-of-the-art sound and lighting systems fit for performances by such legends as Celine Dion, Jerry Seinfeld and Sting. Thanks to the circular layout, there's hardly a bad seat in the house, with no seats further than 145ft from the stage. (☎866-227-5938; www.thecolosseum.com; Caesars Palace; tickets $55-500; 🚌Deuce)

Carrot Top
COMEDY

Even if his ubiquitous presence in the 90s annoyed you to death,

Dressing for Vegas

Dress to impress, whether you're 40-something and doing the rounds of celebrity chefs, or a youngster hitting Drai's beach club. Ladies, you want to look ravishing. Guys, you need to look schmick. Dress codes (collared shirts for men, and no athletic wear or hats) often exist and are enforced. If you want to explore the Strip, wear comfortable shoes. Also, bring loose, cool clothing for the summer heat. Vegas is warm to hot for much of the year, but it can get cold quickly in fall and winter, so be prepared.

this wild and curly, orange-haired comedian's shtick could leave your side split and your gut busted. The fast-paced show (see 10 ⊙ Map p70, C7) runs the audience ragged with physical props, dark and twisted stand-up humor and merciless skewering of pop stars, Hollywood celebs and politicians. (🖉702-262-4400; www.luxor.com; Luxor; tickets $40; ⊗8pm Wed-Mon)

Shopping

Shops at Crystals
MALL

37 🔒 MAP P70, C6

Anchored by a three-story sculptural 'treehouse', Crystals is the Strip's most striking shopping center. If you're feeling flush after winning big at blackjack, you could treat yourself to that new Hermes bag, vertigo-inducing Louboutins or perhaps a flirty Dior dress at Aria's (p52) shrine to haute couture. (www.simon.com/mall/the-shops-at-crystals; 3720 S Las Vegas Blvd, CityCenter; ⊗11am-7pm Mon-Sat, noon-6pm Sun; 🚍Deuce, 🚋Crystals)

Fashion Show
MALL

38 🔒 MAP P70, C4

Nevada's largest shopping mall is an eye-catcher: topped off by 'the Cloud,' a silver multimedia canopy resembling a flamenco hat, Fashion Show harbors more than 250 chain shops and department stores. Live runway shows happen hourly from noon to 5pm on select weekends. (🖉702-369-8382; www.thefashionshow.com; 3200 S Las Vegas Blvd; ⊗10am-9pm Mon-Sat, 11am-7pm Sun; 👫)

Shops at Cosmopolitan

FASHION

39 🔒 MAP P70, C6

Hipster-loving boutiques gather inside the Cosmopolitan (p53) resort: CRSVR sneaker boutique, AllSaints Spitalfields from the UK, Molly Brown's swimwear, Retrospecs & Co eyewear, and Skins 6|2 Cosmetics (if you're a woman, beware of negging from the latter's salespeople). (www.cosmopolitanlasvegas.com/shopping; Cosmopolitan; ☉10am-11pm)

The Forum Shops at Caesars

MALL

40 🔒 MAP P70 C5,

Caesars' (p73) fanciful nod to ancient Roman marketplaces houses 160 designer emporia, including such catwalk classics as Balenciaga, Chanel and Jimmy Choo along with more contemporary brands like Agent Provocateur lingerie and Inglot cosmetics. If that's beyond your budget, steer towards high-street retailers like Guess, Gap and H&M. Don't miss the spiral escalator, a grand entrance for divas strutting off the Strip. (📋702-893-4800; www.simon.com/mall/the-forum-shops-at-caesars-palace; 3500 Las Vegas Blvd S, Caesars Palace; ☉10am-11pm Sun-Thu, to midnight Fri & Sat; 🛜; 🚌Deuce)

Miracle Mile Shops

MALL

41 🔒 MAP P70, C6

This sleekly redesigned shopping mall is a staggering 1.2 miles long. With 170 retailers, the focus is on

Fashion Show

Gangster History

In 1941, Los Angles hotelier Thomas Hull opened Vegas' first casino hotel, El Rancho Vegas, inspiring mobster Benjamin 'Bugsy' Siegel to build an even more luxurious resort in the desert that would draw high rollers from all over the world.

Bugsy & the Flamingo

Backed by East Coast mob money, Siegel took over LA-nightclub owner and *Hollywood Reporter*-publisher Billy Wilkerson's bankrupt construction project and opened the $6 million Flamingo casino hotel in 1946. With its pastel paint job, tuxedo-clad janitors, Hollywood entertainers and flashing neon signs, the Flamingo became the model for the Las Vegas high life to come.

The Fabulous Fifties

In 1950, following a lavish opening party for the Desert Inn (primarily owned by Moe Dalitz, head of a Cleveland-based crime syndicate), a full-blown federal investigation made a disturbing trend crystal clear: the Vegas casino industry had deep ties to mobsters from across the nation. The mob loved Las Vegas. It gave them a legitimacy and a glamorous cachet they had never experienced before. And by fixing the games, bribing local politicians and skimming profits both under and over the table, they were getting rich fast.

Frank Sinatra and his Rat Pack pals helped build this town. They weren't merely legendary headliners; they were also the darlings of gossip columns from LA to New York, and their all-night partying and tumultuous lives entertained millions. Their antics at the Sands casino hotel brought adoring fans, movie stars and famous politicians to Las Vegas by the planeload.

From Mobsters to Megaresorts

In the 1960s, federal and state regulators made an effort to clean up the gambling industry. Scandals plagued the casinos, as charges of corruption, racketeering, influence peddling and tax evasion were investigated by federal agencies – all the bad publicity was hurting tourism. Industrialist Howard Hughes and, later, hotshot Steve Wynn added an air of legitimacy to the scene with their investments and construction of new casino resorts.

KIT LEONG/SHUTTERSTOCK ©

Bonanza Gift Shop

contemporary chains, especially urban apparel, jewelry and gifts. (📞702-866-0704; www.miraclemile shopslv.com; Planet Hollywood; 🕙10am-11pm Sun-Thu, to midnight Fri & Sat)

Houdini's Magic Shop TOYS

42 🅐 MAP P70, C6

Let yourself be roped into this real-deal magic shop by the staff who perform illusions and card tricks out front for sometimes inebriated passersby (they're easy targets). Magician memorabilia and DIY magic kits are sold inside. Check the website for other locations in Vegas. (📞702-798-4789; www.houdini.com; Miracle Mile Shops; 🕙9am-midnight Sun-Thu, to 1am Fri & Sat)

Bonanza Gift Shop GIFTS & SOUVENIRS

43 🅐 MAP P70, D1

The self-proclaimed 'purveyors of Las Vegas pop culture' brag about running the world's largest gift shop. Whether or not it's true, it's a blast wading through the truly terrible, 100% tacky selection of souvenirs. Beware that prices for kitsch are higher here than at Downtown's **Fremont Street Experience** (📞702-678-5600; www. vegasexperience.com; Fremont St Mall; admission free; 🕙24hr, shows hourly dusk-midnight or 1am; 🅿🚻; 🚌Deuce, SDX). (📞702-385-7359; www.worldslargestgiftshop.com; 2440 S Las Vegas Blvd; 🕙8am-11pm)

Explore ◉

East of the Strip

Visits east reward explorers with a deeper understanding of what makes Vegas tick. You won't find many top sights here, but there are a few, like collections of vintage pinball machines, rock-and-roll memorabilia and a glimpse into Las Vegas' dark atomic past. You'll also find cheap eats, bars where bartenders drink and LGBTIQ+ haunts.

The Short List

○ **National Atomic Testing Museum (p94)** Delving into Sin City's dark atomic past.

○ **Pinball Hall of Fame (p98)** Figuring out exactly how many restored retro arcade treasures are actually in here.

○ **Lotus of Siam (p99)** Firing up your palate with some of the best Thai food in America.

○ **Commercial Center (p101)** Meandering around this massive (and slightly rough) strip mall, a universe away from the glossy Strip.

○ **Fruit Loop (p101)** Exploring Vegas' inappropriately named and equally loosely bound LGBTIQ+ enclave.

Getting There & Around

🚌 Run east–west and north–south on major streets including Paradise Rd and Swenson St (bus 108), Flamingo Rd (bus 202) and Tropicana Ave (bus 201).

🚗 Around $15, plus tip, to the Strip; $20 to Downtown.

Neighborhood Map on p96

The National Atomic Testing Center (p94) KIT LEONG/SHUTTERSTOCK ©

Top Experience 📷
Learn About the Atomic Age

The National Atomtic Testing Museum focuses on science, technology and the social history of the 'Atomic Age,' which lasted from WWII until atmospheric bomb testing was driven underground in 1961. A worldwide ban on nuclear testing was declared in 1992. Examine Nevada's nuclear past, present and future, from Native American traditions to the environmental legacy of atomic testing today.

◎ MAP P100, D6

📞 702-409-7366

www.nationalatomi
ctestingmuseum.org

755 E Flamingo Rd

adult/child $22/16

🕙 10am-5pm Mon-Sat, from noon Sun

P

🚌 202

Science & Technology Exhibits

As you make your way through the museum's permanent exhibits, take time to inspect at least a few of the 12,000 historical artifacts collected from the earliest days of atomic testing through to nuclear science today. Learn the history of how the first atomic bomb was developed, and also how atmospheric and underground testing differ. An eye-catching gallery of radiation trackers registers the sobering truth about the dangers of nuclear weapons testing.

Cultural Exhibits

This Smithsonian-affiliated museum also explores the influence of atomic testing on society. Displays show what everyday life was like for Americans during the Cold War, when 'duck and cover' nuclear-bomb drills took place in elementary schools and Nevadans watched mushroom clouds bloom over the desert. Contemporary exhibits look at the environmental costs of atomic weapons, as well as Native American perspectives on land use and nuclear power.

Ticket Booth

Near the museum's front entrance, the ticket booth is a replica of a historical guard station from the Nevada Test Site, where atomic bomb testing began in 1951. Some of the museum volunteers who staff the ticket booth once worked at the site.

Nevada National Security Site

Guided bus tours of the **Nevada National Security Site** (☏702-295-0944; www.nnss.gov/pages/PublicAffairsOutreach/NNSStours.html; admission free) depart from the museum, generally at least once a month. You'll usually get to see surviving structures from the 1950s atomic testing era and moon-like craters that are many football fields wide. Apply online for tour reservations as far in advance as possible.

★ Top Tips

o Combine a visit to the museum with some local cheap eats – there's plenty to savor.

o Uber and Lyft are your friends and by far the easiest way to get to the museum and your subsequent destination (lunch nearby?).

o Apply online for tours of the fascinating, high-security Nevada National Security Site as far in advance as possible (weeks or months advised).

✕ Take a Break

Any time is a good time for tapas, and you're less than a mile away from some of the best Spanish and Latin American dining in town, at locals' prices. Make a bee-line for **Firefly** (p98).

East of the Strip

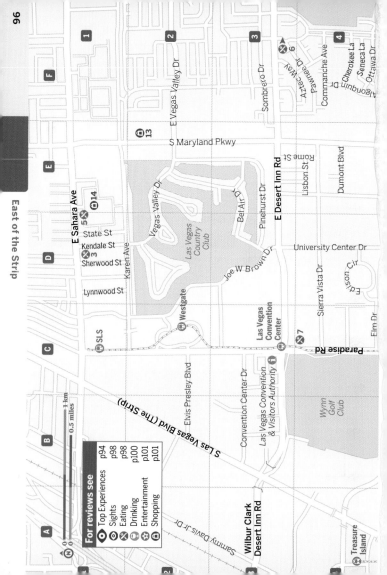

For reviews see

◆ Top Experiences	p94
● Sights	p98
✕ Eating	p98
⊗ Drinking	p100
● Entertainment	p101
⊕ Shopping	p101

0 ————— 1 km
0 ————— 0.5 miles

A B C D E F

1 2 3 4

E Sahara Ave
State St
Kendale St
Sherwood St
Lynnwood St
Karen Ave

SLS
Westgate
SLS

Vegas Valley Dr
Las Vegas Country Club
Bel Air Dr
Pinehurst Dr
Joe W Brown Dr

E Vegas Valley Dr
Sombrero Dr

S Maryland Pkwy

E Desert Inn Rd
Rome St
Lisbon St
Dumont Blvd

University Center Dr

Sierra Vista Dr
Edison Cir
Elm Dr

Las Vegas Convention Center
Las Vegas Convention & Visitors Authority
Paradise Rd

Convention Center Dr

Elvis Presley Blvd

S Las Vegas Blvd (The Strip)

Wynn Golf Club

Sammy Davis Jr Dr

Wilbur Clark Desert Inn Rd

Treasure Island

Pawnee Dr
Azteca Way
Commanche Ave
Cherokee La
Seneca La
Ottawa Dr
Algonquin Dr

5 ✕
14 ⊕
3 ✕
13 ⊕
6 ✕
9 ▲
7 ✕

Sights

Pinball Hall of Fame

MUSEUM

1 ◉ MAP P96, F8

You may have more fun at this no-frills arcade than playing slot machines back on the Strip. Tim Arnold shares his collection of 200-plus vintage pinball and video games with the public. Take time to read the handwritten curatorial cards explaining the unusual history behind these restored machines. (☏702-597-2627; www.pinballmuseum.org; 1610 E Tropicana Ave; per game 25¢-$1; ⊙11am-11pm Sun-Thu, to midnight Fri & Sat; P⛟; 🚌201)

You Can Leave Your Hat On

Vegas is the original adult Disneyland. Sex work may be illegal, but there are plenty of places offering the illusion of sex on demand. Unescorted women are not welcome at most 'gentleman's clubs,' especially not on busy nights. Bring cash for tips. Most strip clubs sit in industrial areas west of the Strip and I-15 Fwy. The largest is Sapphire, with a stable of thousands of entertainers and VIP skyboxes overlooking a showroom dominated by a story-high martini glass. Beefy men strip upstairs on Friday and Saturday nights.

Vegas Mob Tour

BUS

2 ◉ MAP P96, B6

Created with input from real-life mobsters and historians, this bus tour delves into the Mafia underworld of Sin City's past, including celebrity scandals, mobster assassinations and other dirty laundry. Tickets include pizza and admission to Downtown's **Mob Museum** (☏702-229-2734; www.themobmuseum.org; 300 Stewart Ave; adult/student/under 10yr $30/17/free; ⊙9am-9pm; P; 🚌Deuce). By reservation only. (☏702-677-9015; www.vegasmobtour.com; 255 E Flamingo Rd, Tuscany Suites; 3hr tour $100)

Eating

Fat Choy

FUSION $

3 ✖ MAP P96 D1,

Classic American diner meets Asian comfort food in this tiny space within the tidy Eureka locals' casino. (☏702-794-3464; http://fatchoylv.com; 595 E Sahara Ave, Eureka Casino; mains $7-12; ⊙11am-10pm Mon-Thu, to midnight Sat, 9am-10pm Sun)

Firefly

TAPAS $$

4 ✖ MAP P96, C5

Firefly is always packed with a local crowd who come for the Spanish and Latin American tapas, including *patatas bravas*, bacon-wrapped dates and vegetarian bites such as chickpeas seasoned with chili, lime and sea salt. As befits a menu this huge, sometimes the tapas are hit or miss. A backlit bar dispenses the house specialty sangria and fruity mojitos. (📞702-369-3971; www.fireflylv.com; 3824 Paradise Rd; shared plates $5-12, mains $15-32; ⏱11:30am-1am Mon-Thu, to 2am Fri & Sat, 11am-1am Sun; 🚌108)

Lotus of Siam
THAI $$

5 🍴 MAP P96, D1

Saipin Chutima's authentic northern Thai cooking has won almost as many awards as her geographically diverse wine cellar. One bite of her garlic prawns or crispy duck, and you'll be hooked. Although the strip-mall hole-in-the-wall may not look like much,

those in the know flock here. Reservations essential. (📞702-735-3033; www.lotusofsiamlv.com; 620 E Flamingo Rd; mains $9-30; ⏱11am-2:30pm Mon-Fri, 5:30-10pm daily; ❄🛜📶; 🚌202)

Lindo Michoacan
MEXICAN $$

6 🍴 MAP P96, F3

Handmade ceramics and faux adobe walls make this hideout feel far away from the Strip. Family recipes fill the gigantic and satisfying menu of Mexican classics, including seafood, *nopalito* (cactus) salad, beef *lengua* (tongue) and weekend-only *menudo* (tripe and hominy soup). Call ahead for the free shuttle service to/from the convention center's monorail

Pinball Hall of Fame

station. (📞702-735-6828; www.
lindomichoacan.com; 2655 E Desert
Inn Rd; mains $13-24; ⏰10am-11pm;
👶; 🚌203)

Envy

STEAK $$$

7 🍴 MAP P96, C4

A dramatic entrance leads inside
where power brokers recline
against high-backed chairs amid
boldly colored paintings and
theatrical curtains. The signature
steaks and wine cellar get high
marks, with gourmet side dishes
like bourbon creamed corn. It's
next door to the city's convention
center. Reservations recom-
mended. (📞702-784-5700; www.
envysteakhouse.com; 3400 Paradise
Rd, Renaissance Las Vegas; mains
$29-58; ⏰5-10pm; 🚻; 🚇Conven-
tion Center)

Double Down Saloon

This dark, psychedelic gin joint
appeals to the absurd fringe.
Double Down Saloon (📞702-
791-5775; www.doubledownsaloon.
com; 4640 Paradise Rd; ⏰24hr;
🚌108, 202) never closes,
there's never a cover charge,
the house drink is called
'ass juice' and it claims to be
the birthplace of the bacon
martini. When live bands
aren't terrorizing the crowd,
the jukebox vibrates with New
Orleans jazz, British punk,
Chicago blues and surf-guitar
king Dick Dale.

Drinking

Hofbräuhaus

BAR

8 🚇 MAP P96, D7

This Bavarian beer hall and
garden is a replica of the original
in Munich. Celebrate Oktober-
fest year-round with premium
imported suds, fair *Fräuleins* and
live oompah bands nightly. (📞702-
853-2337; www.hofbrauhauslasvegas.
com; 4510 Paradise Rd; ⏰11am-11pm
Sun-Thu, to midnight Fri & Sat)

Garage

LGBTIQ+

9 🚇 MAP P96, F6

One of Vegas' largest and most
popular LGBTIQ+ bars. (📞702-
440-6333; www.thegaragelv.com; 1487
E Flamingo Rd; ⏰24hr)

Piranha

LGBTIQ+

10 🚇 MAP P96, C8

The gay universe orbits the Fruit
Loop's sexiest LGBTIQ+ nightclub,
decked out with fireplace patios,
aquariums and waterfalls, plus the
luxurious 8½ Ultra Lounge. Expect
outrageous theme parties and
drag queen bingo, plus ladies-only
and Latin nights. (📞702-791-0100;
www.piranhavegas.com; 4633 Paradise
Rd; cover weekday/weekend free/$20;
⏰24hr; 🚌108)

Freezone

LGBTIQ+

11 🚇 MAP P96, D7

Every night is a party at this gay
dive bar. Sunday is ladies' night
with go-go girls, Thursday is boyz'

night with go-go boys, Friday and Saturday nights feature drag cabaret, and Tuesday is karaoke. (☎702-794-2300; www.freezonelv. com; 610 E Naples Dr; ⏱24hr; 🚌108)

Entertainment

The Theater
LIVE PERFORMANCE

12 ⭐ MAP P96, C7

Concerts at the Virgin Hotel's scaled-down music venue, holding just 4000 people, feel like private shows, even when rock royalty like the Red Hot Chili Peppers are in town. Intimate acoustic shows happen inside Vinyl lounge (cover charge varies, from nothing up to $40), off the main casino floor. (☎702-693-5000; www.virginhotelslv.com/venue/the-theater; 4455 Paradise Rd, Virgin Hotel; most tickets $40-200; 🚌108)

Shopping

Inyo Fine Cannabis Dispensary
DISPENSARY

13 🔒 MAP P96, E2

One of the first medical marijuana dispensaries in Las Vegas, Inyo has an extensive menu and delivers city-wide. (☎702-707-8888; www. inyolasvegas.com; 2520 Maryland Pkwy #2; ⏱9am-10pm Mon-Thu, to 11pm Fri & Sat, 9am-6pm Sun)

The Fruit Loop
⚢

LGBTIQ+ visitors always ask, 'Where's the gay Strip?' and the answer is always, 'There isn't one,' save for what has been brazenly nicknamed the 'Fruit Loop,' a section of Paradise Rd south of Harmon Ave between Virgin Hotels and the University of Nevada Las Vegas (UNLV), about a mile east of the Strip. There's a gay-centric weighting among the dozen or so bars and clubs comprising its growing-in-fits-and-spurts LGBTIQ+ scene, although a mixed clientele is generally welcomed everywhere, and some haunts do have girls' nights for girls only.

Commercial Center
SHOPPING CENTER

14 🔒 MAP P96, E1

A local institution, this gargantuan and somewhat seedy strip mall is also an endless source of fascination revealing a side of life beyond the Strip. Occupants include two gay saunas, a swingers' joint, a wig shop and various cheap and tasty ethnic restaurants. (☎702-737-3478; www.commercialcenterdistrict. com; 953 E Sahara Ave; ⏱hours vary by business)

Explore ◈
West of the Strip

Why bother heading west of the Strip, you might ask, where the cookie-cutter suburbs rolling onto the Spring Mountains are only interrupted by a casino or three and a dozen strip joints. Well, how about a sky-high zipline, an eco-minded desert oasis and the bustling Chinatown Plaza and suddenly you've got plenty of reasons to head west.

The Short List

○ **Springs Preserve (p104)** Enjoying these educational, meticulously maintained botanical gardens.

○ **Nevada State Museum (p105)** Visiting this educational, eco-friendly and unique museum, where there's dinosaur and mobster stuff to entertain the kids.

○ **Palms (p108)** Frolicking and celebrity-spotting at this off-Strip playpen, with pool parties, posh nosh and sky-high nightclubs for the young and fun.

○ **VooDoo ZipLine (p108)** Daring to ride this jaw-dropping zip line, suspended between Rio's two hotel towers, 500ft above ground.

Getting There & Around

🚌 Run east–west and north–south on major streets, including Tropicana Ave (bus 201), Flamingo Rd (202) and through Chinatown on Spring Mountain Rd (203).

Shuttle Free shuttles run between Rio and Harrah's and Bally's/Paris Las Vegas on the Strip and between the Orleans and Gold Coast casinos.

🚗 One-way fares to the Strip average $10 to $20, to Downtown $20 to $25 (plus tips).

🚶 Unpleasant in this neighborhood due to the dust, heat and long stretches of strip-mall nothing.

Neighborhood Map on p106

Chinatown, Las Vegas (p108) KIT LEONG/SHUTTERSTOCK ©

Top Experience
Visit an Oasis in the Desert

When you just need to get some fresh air and get off the Strip, but don't want to travel too far, Springs Preserve is your best bet. It's situated on the site where now-dry natural springs once fed las vegas (Spanish for 'the meadows'), and southern Paiutes and Old Spanish Trail traders set up camp. It's a literal oasis in the desert and one of Vegas' truly kid-friendly attractions.

702-822-7700
www.springspreserve.org
333 S Valley View Blvd
adult/child $19/11
9am-5pm

104

Origen Museum

Visitors who want to dig beneath the surface of this desert oasis should start at the Origen Museum. The Natural Mojave gallery simulates flash floods and shows the variety of wildlife in the desert. The 'People of the Springs' exhibit narrates Las Vegas' history, from Native American dwellings to the arrival of the railroad and construction of the Hoover Dam. The New Frontier rooms are full of interactive games and kid-friendly activities about conservation, the environment and life in the modern-day city.

Desert Living Center

Nevada's first platinum-certified LEED (Leadership in Energy and Environmental Design) buildings have been constructed from recycled materials and with rammed-earth walls, with passive cooling, renewable heating, reclaimed water and solar-electricity panels, all harvesting clean energy and exemplifying the green future of sustainable design. Inside are classrooms, learning labs and family-oriented exhibits such as the 'Compost Crawl' and 'Garbage Truck Theater.'

Nevada State Museum

Inside the state's natural and cultural history **museum** (📞702-486-5205; www.nvculture.org/nevadastatemuseumlasvegas/; 309 S Valley View Blvd; adult/child $19/11; ⏰9am-5pm Tue-Sun; 🚹), explore more educational exhibits including prehistoric skeletons such as Nevada's state fossil (the ichthyosaur *Shonisaurus popularis*), a replica of a stalactite cave, an atomic explosion display and exhibits covering Sin City's glamorous bygone days.

Gardens & Trails

Almost 4 miles of nature trails are signposted with interpretive displays piecing together Nevada's legacy, from Native Americans to Western pioneers. Take a train ride or rent a bike on weekends to explore them.

★ Top Tips

○ Uber and Lyft rideshare services take the hassle and expense out of travel to and from the park.

○ Plan your day. There are lots of great cheap eats not too far from the park, but decide where to go in advance to save time on the day and help keep those hungry kids happy.

○ For an all-out nature day, combine a park visit with a half-day trip to Red Rock Canyon (best if you have your own wheels).

✂ Take a Break

Lovers of authentic Japanese food without the celebrity Strip treatment will want to round out the day with dinner at **Raku** (📞702-367-3511; www.raku-grill.com/grill; 5030 W Spring Mountain Rd; shared plates $5-20; ⏰6pm-3am Mon-Sat; 🚌203), easily one of Las Vegas' best restaurants.

West of the Strip

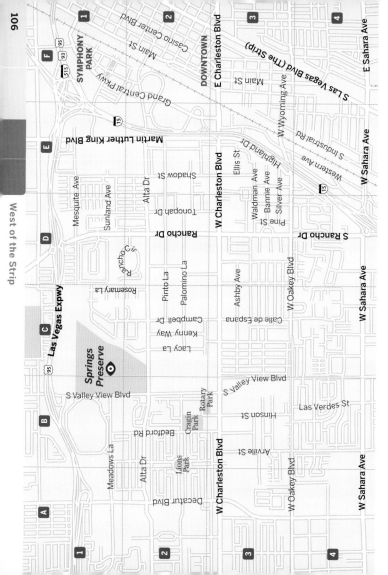

Las Vegas Expwy 95

SYMPHONY PARK

F 515 93 95

Casino Center Blvd

Main St

Grand Central Pkwy

DOWNTOWN

E Charleston Blvd

S Las Vegas Blvd (The Strip)

Main St

W Wyoming Ave

S Industrial Rd

Western Ave

Highland Dr

E Sahara Ave

W Sahara Ave

Martin Luther King Blvd

Mesquite Ave

Sunland Ave

Alta Dr

Shadow St

Tonopah Dr

W Charleston Blvd

Ellis St

Waldman Ave

Bannie Ave

Silver Ave

Pine St

Rancho Cir

Rosemary La

Pinto La

Palomino La

Campbell Dr

Rancho Dr

Ashby Ave

Calle de España

W Oakey Blvd

S Rancho Dr

Kenny Way

Lacy La

Springs Preserve

S Valley View Blvd

Rotary Park

S Valley View Blvd

Las Verdes St

Meadows La

Alta Dr

Bedford Rd

Cr006in Park

Lions Park

Decatur Blvd

W Charleston Blvd

Hinson St

Arville St

W Oakey Blvd

W Sahara Ave

West of the Strip

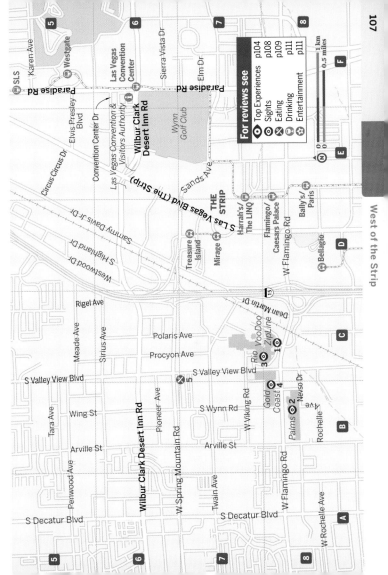

Karen Ave

⊙ SLS

Westgate 5

Paradise Rd

Las Vegas Convention Center 6

Sierra Vista Dr

Elm Dr

7

Paradise Rd

Elvis Presley Blvd

Convention Center Dr

Las Vegas Convention & Visitors Authority

Wilbur Clark Desert Inn Rd

Wynn Golf Club

8

For reviews see

◉ Top Experiences — p104
◉ Sights — p108
✕ Eating — p109
🍷 Drinking — p111
✸ Entertainment — p111

Ⓝ

0 —— 1 km
0 —— 0.5 miles

E   F

Circus Circus Dr

Sammy Davis Jr Dr

Sands Ave

THE STRIP
S Las Vegas Blvd (The Strip)

Harrah's/
The LINQ

Flamingo/
Caesars Palace

W Flamingo Rd

Bally's/
Paris

Westwood Dr

S Highland Dr

Treasure Island

Mirage

W Flamingo Rd

Bellagio

D

Rigel Ave

Meade Ave

Sirius Ave

Tara Ave

Wing St

Arville St

Penwood Ave

W Spring Mountain Rd

Polaris Ave

Procyon Ave

S Valley View Blvd

Pioneer Ave

Arville St

Dean Martin Dr

15

Rio

VooDoo
ZipLine

1

Gold Coast

3

5

S Valley View Blvd

S Wynn Rd

W Viking Rd

4

Palms

2

Nevso Dr

Ave

Rochelle

C

Twain Ave

Wilbur Clark Desert Inn Rd

S Decatur Blvd

W Flamingo Rd

S Decatur Blvd

W Rochelle Ave

A   B

5   6   7   8

Sights

VooDoo ZipLine

ADVENTURE SPORTS

1 ◉ MAP P106, C8

How does 'flying' between Rio's two hotel towers sound? The ride starts with you strapped into a seat on a 50-story tower. Four hundred feet below is the expansive pool area, and beyond is the cityscape. Once the operator sets you free, you'll whiz down metal lines to a lower tower, taking in the 800ft-long rush...then get pulled back! The ticket price includes entry into the adjacent VooDoo Rooftop Nightclub. (☑702-388-0477; www.voodoo zipline.com; Rio; from $25; ☺11am-midnight)

Chinatown Las Vegas

Head west from the Strip along Spring Mountain Rd and you'll find yourself in the heart of Las Vegas' strip-mall Chinatown. Slightly off the tourist radar, **Chinatown Plaza** (☑702-221-8448; 4255 Spring Mountain Rd; most mains $6-18; ☺hours vary; 🚻; 🚌203) is a favorite with local foodies for its late-night Vietnamese noodle shops, Japanese sushi bars, Korean barbecue grills and more. Start exploring at this plaza with an eye-catching Chinese gate.

Palms

CASINO

2 ◉ MAP P106, B8

The ultramodern Palms casino hotel burns brightly with a mix of entertainment designed to seduce gen-Xers and -Yers. Infamous for its starring role on MTV's *Real World: Las Vegas* reality TV series, the Palms has a high-drama, neon-lit atmosphere that's equal parts sexy and sleazy. With some of the best odds near the Strip, the casino ropes in plenty of tourists and locals too. (☑702-942-7770; www.palms.com; 4321 W Flamingo Rd; ☺24hr; 🚌202)

Rio

CASINO

3 ◉ MAP P106, C8

Despite its Carnaval theme, the all-suites Rio casino hotel is often overshadowed by the action at the Palms casino resort across the street. Occupying most of its corny two-story 'Masquerade Village' is a 100,000 square foot casino decked out with a colorful motif and more than 1200 slot machines, 80 table games, a full-service race and sports book with 100 TVs and a cut-throat poker room that's home to the **World Series of Poker** (www.wsop.com; Rio; ☺May-Jul) finals. (☑866-746-7671; www.riolasvegas.com; 3700 W Flamingo Rd; ☺24hr; 🚌free Strip shuttle)

Gold Coast

CASINO

4 ◉ MAP P106, B8

The neighborhood west of the Strip has several old-school casino

Frontier Days

For many hundreds of years, Southern Paiute tribespeople lived a relatively peaceful if arduous existence in the desert around the present-day Las Vegas Valley. They were the descendants of Paiutes, one of the Native American tribes who lived near the Grand Canyon along the Colorado River. Their undoing as the dominant people of the region began with the arrival of Europeans.

Discovering the Springs

In 1829 Rafael Rivera, a scout for a Mexican trading expedition, was likely the first outsider to locate the natural springs in this valley, which Spanish colonists called *las vegas* ('the meadows'). Another traveler along the Old Spanish Trail, US Army officer John C Fremont, arrived in 1844 to explore and map the area. (Las Vegas' main downtown artery, Fremont St, bears his name today.)

The Mormon 'Invasion'

Amid the legions of miners who arrived later in the mid-19th century was a group hell-bent on doing God's work. These Mormons were sent from Salt Lake City by church leader Brigham Young to colonize the state of Deseret, their spiritual homeland. In 1855 the Mormons built a fort near what is now downtown Las Vegas, but abandoned it less than two years later. After the US Civil War (1861–65), small farms and ranches flourished in the Las Vegas Valley.

Arrival of the Railroad

On January 30, 1905, a railroad linking Salt Lake City with Los Angeles was completed in southern Nevada at a place called Jean, only 25 miles from Las Vegas. Later that year, during two days in mid-May, pioneers and real-estate speculators from LA bid for land in the newly established Las Vegas townsite, with some lots being auctioned off for up to 10 times their original asking price.

hotels, such as Gold Coast – now as well known for its authentic Chinese cuisine as its gaming tables and slot machines that target locals, retirees and the package-tour crowd. (☏702-367-7111; www.goldcoastcasino.com; 4000 W Flamingo Rd; ⏱24hr; 🚌202)

Eating

Hot n Juicy Crawfish

SEAFOOD $$

5 ⊗ MAP P106, C6

The name says it all: spicy, hot and juicy crawfish served by the pound or in baskets and a wide range of other seafood treats. Ridiculously popular. There's another location at 3863 Spring Mountain Rd, conveniently close to Golden Tiki. (📞702-891-8889; www.hotnjuicycrawfish.com; 4810 Spring Mountain Rd; baskets $12-20; 🕐noon-10pm Sun-Thu, to 11pm Fri & Sat; P🥢👪)

Ping Pang Pong CHINESE $$

Asian package tourists and Chinatown locals vote with their feet, and it's always crowded here (see 4 📍 Map p106, B8). Designed by chef Kevin Wu, a wok-tossed menu ranges across the regions of China, from Beijing seafood stew to Shanghai noodles to Cantonese sausage fried rice. The dim sum carts roll until 3pm daily. (📞702-367-7111; www.goldcoastcasino.com; 4000 W Flamingo Rd, Gold Coast; mains $10-24; 🕐10am-3pm & 5pm-3am; 🚌202)

Carnival World & Seafood Buffet BUFFET $$$

Las Vegas' largest all-around buffet (see 3 📍 Map p106, C8) is found at Rio (p108), with stir-fries, pizza, a taco bar and housemade gelato. There's a $15 seafood add-on for those who can't get enough snow crab legs, lobster tails and freshly shucked oysters. (📞702-777-7757; www.riolasvegas.com; Rio; per person $25-35; 🕐11am-10pm; 👪; 🚌free Strip shuttle)

Ping Pang Pong

KIT LEONG/SHUTTERSTOCK ©

Drinking

VooDoo Rooftop Nightclub
CLUB

The distant views of the Strip's neon glow from the outdoor patio are fantastic, but the DayGlo decor and DJs inside are just for laughs (see 3 ⊙ Map p106, C8). An unpretentious crowd dances to old-school, retro and techno tunes while swigging exotic, oversized cocktails steaming with dry ice. Retirees and buttoned-down conventioneers let loose here. (☎702-777-6875; www. caesars.com/rio-las-vegas; Rio; cover $10-30; ⊙8pm-2am Sun-Thu, to 3am Fri & Sat; ☐free Strip shuttle)

Entertainment

Penn & Teller
COMEDY

Rio's (p108) star performers (see 3 ⊙ Map p106, C8), this intellectual odd couple (one talks, the other doesn't) has been creating and destroying illusions for more than two decades, with dry wit, peppery profanity and some amazing stunts such as catching bullets in their teeth. The gimmick? They explain some (but not all) of their tricks to the audience. Stick around after the show for autographs and selfies. (☎702-777-2782; www.pennandteller.com; Rio; tickets from $74; ⊙9pm Sat-Wed; ☐free Strip shuttle)

Frankie's Tiki Room

At this round-the-clock tiki bar, insanely inventive tropical cocktails are rated in strength by skulls on the menu. Renowned tiki designers, sculptors and painters have their work on display all around **Frankie's Tiki Room** (☎702-385-3110; www.frankiestikiroom. com; 1712 W Charleston Blvd; ⊙24hr; ☐206), and the souvenir tiki mugs are crazy cool. Walk in wearing a Hawaiian shirt on 'Aloha Friday' between 4pm and 8pm, and your first drink is half-off.

Pearl
THEATER

A shining beacon for pop divas and rock bands, the Palms' (p108) 2500-seat concert hall (see 2 ⊙ Map p106, B8) has a sophisticated sound system. Comedy kingpins and modern rockers from Gwen Stefani to Morrissey have burned up this stage, with many seats only 120ft or less away from the performers. Live albums are minted at the state-of-the-art recording studio. (☎702-944-3200; www.palms. com; 4321 W Flamingo Rd, Palms; most tickets $50-100; ☐202)

Explore ⬡

Downtown &

Fremont Street

With the retro casinos of the Fremont Street Experience, the vibrant Arts and Fremont East Entertainment Districts, cheap digs, cool museums

The Short List

○ **Golden Nugget (p114)** *Enjoying this glittering 1946 casino's star attractions, including the world's largest golden nugget and a 200,000-gallon shark tank.*

○ **Mob Museum (p116)** *Visiting Las Vegas' old federal courthouse, which now houses this cutting-edge collection that traces the development of organized crime in early America.*

○ **Container Park (p123)** *Shopping at this edgy incubator for up-and-coming fashion designers and local artisans.*

○ **Neon Museum (p125)** *Admiring this museum's vintage neon signs, dating from the 1930s onward.*

○ **Vintage shopping in the Arts District** (☎702-384-2700; www.retro-vegas.com; 1131 S Main St; ⊙11am-6pm Mon-Sat, noon-5pm Sun; 🚌108, Deuce) *Digging for silver (this is Nevada, remember?) through the racks of bowling shirts, gold-rimmed martini glasses and neon signs.*

Getting There & Around

🚌 Deuce & SDX head to and from the Strip. The free Downtown Loop Bus has convenient stops throughout Downtown.

🚗 $15 to $25 one way (plus tip) to or from the Strip.

Neighborhood Map on p124

Top Experience 📷
Strike Gold at a Classy Old-School Casino

Day or night, the Golden Nugget is Downtown's poshest address. With classy eateries and a swimming pool famous for its shark tank, it outshines the competition. This swank joint rakes in a moneyed crowd with a 38,000-sq-ft casino populated by table games and slot machines with the same odds as at Strip megaresorts. The non-smoking poker room hosts daily tournaments.

◉
☎ 702-385-7111
www.goldennugget.com
129 Fremont St E
🕐 24hr
🅿 🚻
🚌 Deuce, SDX

Hand of Faith

The Golden Nugget's namesake claim to fame is the Hand of Faith. It's not a religious relic, but the heftiest hunk of gold ever found, weighing a massive 61lb 11oz (28kg). Discovered in Australia, it's now on display under glass near the North Tower elevators.

Shark Tank

Slip outside onto the pool terrace to gawk at the enormous shark tank – be sure to walk around to the back side for the best views. Yes, those are hotel guests hurtling through the aquarium: an innovative enclosed water slide spirals down three stories through the tank, providing a unique aquatic experience for thrill-seekers.

Casino

Check out the polished brass and white leather seats in the Golden Nugget's casino: day or night, this is Downtown's poshest address. The airy, nonsmoking poker room stages daily poker tournaments.

Chart House

If you dig the shark tank, get a load of the Golden Nugget's other creatively positioned aquarium. Vegas' branch of the high-end **Chart House** (☏702-386-8364; www.chart-house.com/locations/las-vegas/; 129 Fremont St E, Golden Nugget; mains $23-45; ⏱11:30am-midnight Sun-Thu, to 1am Fri & Sat) chain eatery is anchored by a stunning 75,000-gallon aquarium and serves a variety of aquatic delights from Alaskan sea bass to coconut shrimp prepared practically any way you like.

★ Top Tips

○ For a closer look at the Shark Tank, take a behind-the-scenes tour ($30).

○ For a peek at some smaller fry, stop for a drink at Chart House, a seafood restaurant where you can perch at the bar encircling a 75,000-gallon tropical aquarium.

✖ Take a Break

Nip around the corner and check out the expansive urban oasis that is **Gold Spike** (p121); with its playroom, living room and backyard, there's something for everyone.

Otherwise, for a sunny beverage and bar snacks, head to the northeast corner of Fremont and Las Vegas Blvd and grab a patio seat at **Park on Fremont** (☏702-834-3160; www.parkonfremont. com; 506 Fremont St E; light meals $10-15; ⏱11am-3am).

Top Experience 📷
Soak up the City's Mob History

Opened to great fanfare on February 14, 2012 – the 83rd anniversary of the notorious St Valentine's Day Massacre in Chicago – the Mob Museum's official name is the National Museum of Organized Crime & Law Enforcement. Even the museum's physical location is impressive, inside a historic US federal courthouse where mobsters sat for hearings in 1950–51.

👁

📞 702-229-2734

www.themobmuseum.org

300 Stewart Ave

adult/student/under 10yr $30/17/free

🕐 9am-9pm

🅿

🚌 Deuce

Mob Museum Exhibits

With a board of directors headed up by a former FBI Special Agent, this museum takes its sensationalist subject seriously. Thoughtfully curated exhibits tell the story of organized crime in America from the perspective of both gangsters and coppers. In addition to hands-on FBI equipment and mob-related artifacts, the museum boasts a series of multimedia exhibits featuring interviews with real-life Tony Sopranos.

Mob Museum Theater

Break up your journey through the museum's exhibits by plonking yourself down in a plush theater seat to watch videos projected on the big screen. If you're looking for History Channel–style documentaries, you'll be disappointed – most of the clips being shown are classic Hollywood gangster movies.

Gift Shop

The Mob Museum gift shop is a trove of offbeat Sin City souvenirs, whether you're on the hunt for a gangster fedora, a spy pen that writes with ultraviolet ink or a coffee mug with a handle made of brass knuckles. On a nerdy note, the shop fills its bookshelves with respectable tomes on the history of Sin City and the American Mafia.

Historic Architecture

Listed on the National Register of Historic Places, the building that houses the museum was built in 1933 and was once the Las Vegas post office and courthouse. It's one of the oldest buildings in Las Vegas, a city that only really got started as recently as 1905. On the proviso that it be restored and used for cultural purposes, the federal police, who operated the courthouse, sold the building in 2002 to the City of Las Vegas for the princely sum of $1!

★ **Top Tips**

o The museum extends its educational mission by hosting special events, such as author readings and talks on everything from true-crime stories to casino cheating.

o Fascinating panel discussions take place inside the historic courtroom.

✕ **Take a Break**

Head down to nearby **Evel Pie** (📞702-840-6460; http://evelpie.com; 508 Fremont St E; pizza slices $4-5.50, whole pies $26-28; 🕐11am-2am Sun-Wed, to 4:20am Thu-Sat) for a slice of mobster-y pizza.

Directly opposite you'll find **Flippin' Good Burgers & Fries** (📞702-776-7991; http://flippingood.com; 505 Fremont St E; burgers $11; 🕐11am-11pm Sun-Thu, to 2am Fri & Sat) where the burgers are...well, you know how this ends.

Walking Tour

Downtown Wander

With the retro casinos of the Fremont Street Experience, vibrant hipster and art districts, affordable eats, cool museums and free entertainment galore, a stroll around Downtown is a great antidote to all that Strip glamour madness. You'll make the acquaintance of mobsters, marvel at a giant gold nugget, visit an edgy incubator for artists and designers, and be dazzled by vintage neon and a blazing sound-and-light after-dusk show.

Walk Facts

Start Mob Museum

End Plaza

Length 0.9 miles; one to two hours

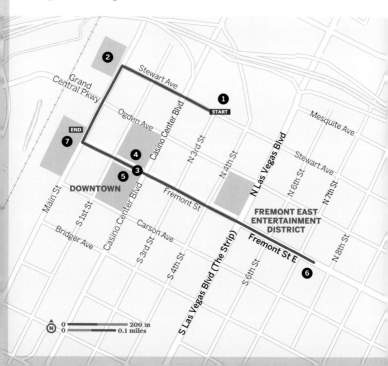

❶ Mob Museum

Take a stroll through Fremont St, stopping off in old-time casinos and hipster dive bars before visiting the thought-provoking **Mob Museum** (p116) for an overview of organized crime in the USA from the turn of the 20th century to the present.

❷ Main Street Station

Head west on Stewart Ave to **Main Street Station** (p127) for a self-guided tour of the eclectic antiques collection. Continue south on Main St past the rail car once owned by Wild West showman Buffalo Bill.

❸ Fremont Street Experience

Walk east through the heart of Glitter Gulch, Vegas' original gambling quarter, reborn in 1995 as the **Fremont Street Experience** (p128). Adventure seekers whoosh overhead on the **SlotZilla** (p127) zipline, taking note of the unmissable neon icon Vegas Vicky.

❹ Binion's Gambling Hall

Step inside historic **Binion's** (p126) to check out the action in the high-stakes poker room and watch real-life cowboys and cowgirls try their luck at blackjack.

❺ Golden Nugget

Cross Fremont St to the classy **Golden Nugget** (p114). Ogle the gigantic Hand of Faith just off the casino floor, then slip outside onto the pool terrace to gawk at the enormous shark tank – the best views are from the back side.

❻ Container Park

Keep going east toward the glowing neon martini glass welcoming you to the Fremont East Entertainment District, home to hipster watering holes such as **Commonwealth** (☏702-445-6400; www.common-wealthlv.com; 525 Fremont St; ⏱7pm-late Tue-Sat, 10pm-late Sun; 🚌Deuce) and the indie shops and eateries of the **Container Park** (p123).

❼ Plaza

Head west back up Fremont St and wind up your walk at the revamped **Plaza** (p126), imagining what pioneer life was like when the adjacent former Union Pacific Railroad auctioned off dusty lots here in 1905. Head upstairs to Oscar's steakhouse and martini lounge for flight-deck views over the Fremont Street Experience.

✕ Take a Break

Carson Kitchen (☏702-473-9523; www.carsonkitchen.com; 124 S 6th St; tapas & mains $8-22; ⏱11:30am-11pm Thu-Sat, to 10pm Sun-Wed; ❄🛜🚌Deuce) Make a pit stop in this tiny industrial-flavored eatery to refuel on modern American share plates.

Walking Tour 🥾

Downtown Arts District Walk

Making a masterpiece takes time, and Downtown's Arts District remains a work in progress: a hodgepodge of artist studios, compact galleries, quirky street art and storefronts – no wonder it's the epicenter of the monthly **First Friday** *(p126) parties. It's also one of the few 'walk-friendly' spots in the city, despite retaining a gritty true-to-its-roots charm.*

Walk Facts

Start Gold Spike

End Esther's Kitchen

Length 1.6 miles; three hours

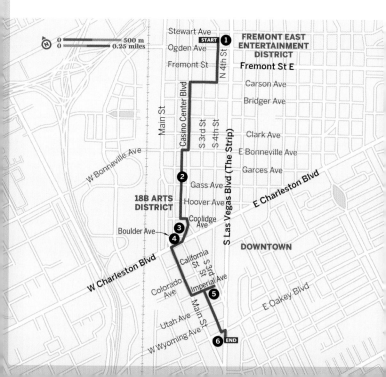

❶ Gold Spike

Gold Spike (📞702-476-1082; www.goldspike.com; 217 N Las Vegas Blvd; ⏰24hr), with its playroom, living room and backyard, is many things: bar, nightclub, performance space, work space; sometime host of roller derbies, discos, live bands or dance parties; or just somewhere to soak up the sun with a relaxed crew and escape mainstream Vegas. If you love it like the locals do, you can even spend the night in the **Oasis at Gold Spike** (📞702-768-9823; www.oasisatgoldspike.com; 217 N Las Vegas Blvd; weekend d from $148; 🅿❄☠).

❷ Street Art Central

The alleyway between S 1st St and S Casino Blvd, between Bonneville Ave and Charleston Ave, is home to plenty of good graffiti, although you'll find the entire Arts District and the area around Fremont East to be a veritable living gallery of street art, including entire buildings and stories-high works by some of the world's best street artists.

❸ Boutiques & Burlesque

The Arts District (also known by locals as '18b,' as it was planned to be 18 blocks of art...nobody is sure how many it actually is) is full of original boutiques, vintage stores, pop-up shops and clearance outlets, and it's constantly changing. Check out **Buffalo Exchange** (p131) and **Rainbow Feather** (p131) for inspiration before dropping in on the **Burlesque Hall of Fame** (p127).

❹ Art Square & Art Factory

Side by side, **Art Square** (📞702-300-4337; www.dtlvarts.com/art-square; 1017 & 1025 S 1st St; ⏰office hours 11am-5pm Mon-Fri, gallery hours vary; 🚌Deuce, SDX) and the **Arts Factory** (📞702-383-9907; www.theartsfactory.com; 107 E Charleston Blvd; ⏰9am-6pm; 🚌Deuce, SDX) form the undisputed hub of the Arts District. Once a block of derelict buildings and warehouses, this is now ground zero for **First Fridays**, when thousands roam around the vibrant area on the first Friday evening of every month.

❺ Bars, Bunnies and Bric-a-Brac

It's Vegas, so any time is a good time for some bar hopping. After all this walking, shopping and chatting with the locals, you're bound to be thirsty. So what's your flavor? If you're LGBTIQ+ friendly, pop in to Bastille on 3rd, Vegas' first gay bar; the **Velveteen Rabbit** (p129) for arty mixology; or **ReBAR** (p130) if you're a mad vintage fan.

❻ Celebrate Carbs

You reserved ahead, right? **Esther's Kitchen** (📞702-570-7864; www.estherslv.com; 1130 S Casino Center Blvd; pasta from $15; ⏰11am-3pm & 5-10pm Mon-Fri, from 10am Sat & Sun; ❄🛜) isn't helmed by a celebrity chef, but it's the hottest table in the Arts District. Super authentic, well-priced Italian pastas, pizzas and small plates are just the ticket after a long day wandering in the heat.

Walking Tour 🚶

Fremont East Food & Booze Ramble

The section of Fremont St east of Las Vegas Blvd and the few blocks south, forms the Fremont East Entertainment District, aka 'Fremont East'. Like any good cocktail, it's a highly concentrated jolt of fun and flavor, chock full of party haunts and drinking holes from dive bars to discos; and some of Vegas' most impressive (and chill), niche eateries.

Walk Facts

Start Park on Fremont

End Fremont Country Club

Length 0.5 miles; two to three hours

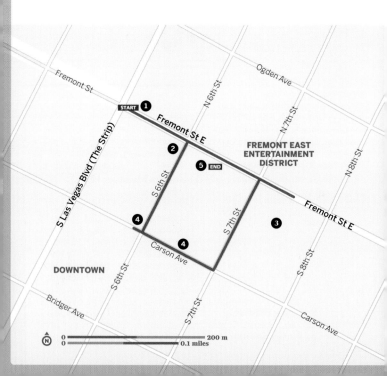

❶ Park on Fremont

If you're already pretty jolly (not that we condone unruly behavior so early in the day), it's only a short stumble to Fremont St E once you hop off the bus from the Strip. Here you'll find **Park on Fremont** (p115), a gastropub with greasy share plates and sunny patios perfect for people watching and planning your next move.

❷ Commonwealth

Commonwealth (☏702-445-6400; www.commonwealthlv.com; 525 Fremont St; ⊙7pm-late Tue-Sat, 10pm-late Sun; 🚌Deuce) has a Prohibition-era interior is worth a look, including plush booths, softly glowing chandeliers, Victorian-era bric-a-brac and a saloon bar. Better still, sip your old-timey cocktails on the rooftop patio overlooking the decidedly more contemporary Fremont East scene. Folks here are a little snooty, but you would be too if you had to walk around with that fancy mustache.

❸ Container Park

An incubator for up-and-coming fashion designers and local artisans by day, **Container Park** (☏702-359-9982; www.downtown containerpark.com; 707 Fremont St; ⊙11am-9pm, food & drink to 11pm Sun-Thu, to 1am Fri & Sat; 🛜; 🚌Deuce) goes adults only (21-plus) after 9pm. When the sun sets, the container bars come to life and host regular themed events and movie nights. With food-truck-style menus, outdoor patio seating and late-night hours, food vendors inside the cutting-edge Container Park sell something to satisfy everyone's appetite.

❹ Line Your Stomach

Health professionals recommend not drinking on an empty stomach, but you've probably already done that, so why not tidy yourself up and hit up **Carson Kitchen** (☏702-473-9523; www.carsonkitchen.com; 124 S 6th St; tapas & mains $8-22; ⊙11:30am-11pm Thu-Sat, to 10pm Sun-Wed; ❄🛜🚌Deuce) for scrumptious share plates or **VegeNation** (☏702-366-8515; https://vegenationlv.com; 616 E Carson Ave; mains $13; ⊙8am-9pm Sun-Thu, to 10pm Fri & Sat; ❄🛜🖊; 🚌Deuce, BHX) for the best vegan food in town. If you're starting early (or out very late), **eat.** (p128) serves one of the best breakfasts you'll find in Vegas.

❺ Catch a Band

It's Vegas, so the night is young (whatever time it is) and there's usually always something going on at the **Fremont Country Club** (☏702-382-6601; www.fremont countryclubvegas.com; 601 Fremont St E; ticket prices vary; ⊙show times vary), a sprawling old-school concert hall in the heart of Fremont East. Check the website for listings: expect anything from rock to alternative, blues to country, punk to pop.

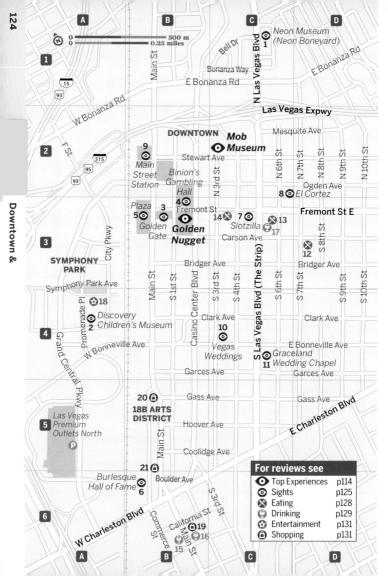

A **B** **C** **D**

1

0 — 500 m
0 — 0.25 miles

Neon Museum
(Neon Boneyard)
1

Bell Dr

Bonanza Way

E Bonanza Rd

N Las Vegas Blvd

E Bonanza Rd

W Bonanza Rd

F St

Main St

E Bonanza Rd

Las Vegas Expwy

2

Mesquite Ave

DOWNTOWN   **Mob Museum**

9

Stewart Ave

Main Street Station

Binion's Gambling Hall

3

Plaza
5

Golden Gate

Fremont St
4

Golden Nugget

14

7

Slotzilla
17

Ogden Ave

N 6th St
N 7th St
N 8th St
N 9th St
N 10th St

El Cortez
8

Fremont St E

13

S 8th St

12

3

SYMPHONY PARK

City Pkwy

Carson Ave

Bridger Ave

Main St

S 1st St

Casino Center Blvd

S 3rd St

S 4th St

S Las Vegas Blvd (The Strip)

S 6th St

S 7th St

Bridger Ave

S 9th St

S 10th St

4

Symphony Park Ave

Promenade Pl

18

Discovery Children's Museum
2

W Bonneville Ave

Clark Ave

10

Vegas Weddings

Clark Ave

Graceland Wedding Chapel
11

E Bonneville Ave

Grand Central Pkwy

Garces Ave

Garces Ave

Garces Ave

5

Las Vegas Premium Outlets North
P

20
18B ARTS DISTRICT

Main St

Gass Ave

Hoover Ave

Coolidge Ave

Gass Ave

E Charleston Blvd

21

Burlesque Hall of Fame
6

Boulder Ave

S 3rd St

6

W Charleston Blvd

Commerce St

California St
19

Main St
16

15

For reviews see

◉	Top Experiences	p114
◉	Sights	p125
✕	Eating	p128
⊖	Drinking	p129
★	Entertainment	p131
⊟	Shopping	p131

A **B** **C** **D**

Sights

Neon Museum

MUSEUM

1 ◉ MAP P124, C1

A cowboy on horseback, Aladdin's genie lamp and a glowing martini glass are among the iconic Vegas neon signs to get a new lease of life at the Neon Boneyard of this non-profit Downtown museum. You're free to wander around the alfresco exhibit (download the free app) or join a one-hour guided tour, preferably after dark. Check-in is inside the rescued lobby of the salvaged La Concha Motel, a shell-shaped jewel by Paul Revere Williams. (☎702-387-6366; www.neonmuseum. org; 770 N Las Vegas Blvd; tickets $20; ☉4pm-midnight; P♿; ☐113)

Discovery Children's Museum

MUSEUM

2 ◉ MAP P124, A4

Designed for toddlers to pre-teens, the Discovery Children's Museum is located in a state-of-the-art building in Symphony Park. Highlights include 'The Summit,' a 12-story tower of interactive activities and play space, plus themed educational and entertaining exhibits such as Eco City, Water World, Toddler Town, Fantasy Festival, Patents Pending and Young at Art. (☎702-382-3445; www. discoverykidslv.org; 360 Promenade Pl, Symphony Park; $14.50; ☉10am-5pm Mon-Sat, from noon Sun Jun-early Sep, 9am-4pm Tue-Fri, noon-5pm Sat & Sun rest of year; ♿; ☐SDX)

Neon Museum

Golden Gate

CASINO

3 〇 MAP P124, B3

A gambling hall and hotel have stood on this corner since 1906, one year after the whistle-stop railway town of Las Vegas was founded. It didn't become the Golden Gate until 1955, when a troupe of Italian Americans from San Francisco decamped and stayed on for four decades to manage what was previously known as the 'Sal Sagev' (the city's name spelled backwards). Today, the Golden Gate's hypnotic sign is almost as irresistible as its famous shrimp cocktails. (📞702-385-1906; www.goldengate-casino.com; 1 Fremont St; ⊘24hr; 🚌Deuce, SDX)

Binion's Gambling Hall

CASINO

4 〇 MAP P124, B3

Binion's Gambling Hall was opened in 1951 (then known as Binion's Horseshoe), by notorious Texan gambler Benny Binion, who wore gold coins for buttons on his cowboy shirts and spurred the transformation of Fremont St casino hotels from sawdust gambling halls to classy carpet joints. Benny was among the first to offer free drinks for slot-machine players and airport limo rides for high rollers. Today, what appeals most about this bedraggled Downtown property is its genuine country-and-western flavor. (📞702-382-1600; www.binions.com; 128 Fremont St E; ⊘24hr; 🚌Deuce, SDX)

First Fridays

On the first Friday evening of each month, Downtown comes to life as art lovers, hipsters, foodies and musicians come out to play in the 18b Arts District and Fremont East Entertainment District. **First Friday** (www.ffflv.org; ⊘5-11pm 1st Friday every month) is like a giant block party, featuring art gallery openings, live music, performance art, children's activities and food trucks selling everything from snow cones to fried pickles.

Plaza

CASINO HOTEL

5 〇 MAP P124, B31

Built on the site of a Union Pacific Railroad Depot, the Plaza opened in 1971. For decades it was a gaudy, cheap-looking hotel attracting package tourists and blue-haired, bingo-playing grandmothers. Although recently renovated with a fresher, more contemporary appearance (think hipsters in '70s getups), the place is far from pretentious – it still packs in loyal gamblers with its rowdy $5 blackjack tables and cocktail waiters who call you 'hun.' (📞702-386-2110; www.plazahotelcasino.com; 1 S Main St; ⊘24hr; 🚌Deuce, SDX)

Burlesque Hall of Fame

MUSEUM

6 ⓞ MAP P124, B6

Housed in the Art Square (p121) complex, this sweet museum pays homage to the history of burlesque performance in the USA. Gawk at fab sequined outfits and photographs of some of the genre's sultriest stars from yesteryear. (📞888-661-6465; www. burlesquehall.com; 1027 South Main Street, Suite 110; $15; ⏱10am-6pm Tue-Sun; 🚌Deuce)

SlotZilla

ADVENTURE SPORTS

7 ⓞ MAP P124, C3

Soar above the glittering Fremont Street Experience (p128) – seated or 'Superman–style' – on two ziplines that launch from a giant slot machine flanked by two neon showgirls. Flights before 5pm cost $5 less. (📞844-947-8342; www. vegasexperience.com/slotzilla-zip-line; Fremont St Mall, Fremont Street Experience; lower/upper line $29/49; ⏱1pm-1am Sun-Thu, to 2am Fri & Sat; 👪; 🚌Deuce, SDX)

El Cortez

CASINO

8 ⓞ MAP P124, C2

Head to the unabashedly retro El Cortez, Vegas' oldest continuously operating casino, on the National Register of Historic Places. Going strong since 1941, it's one of the only carpet joints left where the slot machines are the real thing. If you hit the jackpot, you'll enjoy the clatter of actual coins – none

Main Street Station

of that newfangled paper ticket nonsense. (📞702-385-5200; www. elcortezhotelcasino.com; 600 Fremont St E; ⏱24hr; 🚌Deuce)

Main Street Station

CASINO

9 ⓞ MAP P124, B2

This filigreed casino recreates Victorian opulence with its unique design, detailed craftwork and an extensive antiques collection. Pick up a brochure at the hotel's front desk and take a self-guided tour of the *objets d'histoires*. Highlights include exquisite bronze chandeliers (originally from an 1890s Coca Cola building in Austin, TX), a graffiti-covered chunk of the Berlin Wall (now supporting a urinal in the men's restroom) and an art nouveau chandelier from Paris'

Fremont Street Experience

Streaking down the center of Vegas' Glitter Gulch historical district Downtown, **Fremont Street Experience** (☎702-678-5600; www.vegasexperience.com; Fremont St Mall; admission free; ☺24hr, shows hourly dusk-midnight or 1am; P📶; 🚌Deuce, SDX) is a five-block pedestrian mall lined with old-school casinos and topped by an arched steel canopy. Hourly from dusk until midnight, the 1400ft-long canopy turns on an amiably cheesy six-minute light-and-sound show.

Figaro Opera House. (☎702-387-1896; www.mainstreetcasino.com; 200 N Main St; ☺24hr; 🚌SDX)

Vegas Weddings   CEREMONY

11 ◉ MAP P124, C4

With the only walk-up (and drive-thru) wedding window in Vegas, plus a cathedral-style chapel, this newly built place also arranges weddings at scenic outdoor spots such as **Valley of Fire** (☎702-397-2088; http://parks.nv.gov/parks/valley-of-fire; Valley of Fire Hwy, Overton; per vehicle $10; ☺sunrise-sunset), **Lake Mead** (☎info desk 702-293-8906, visitor center 702-293-8990; www.nps.gov/lake; Lakeshore Scenic Dr; 7-day entry per vehicle $25; ☺24hr; 📶) and the Grand Canyon. (☎702-430-2998; www.702wedding.com; 555 S 3rd St; drive-thru weddings from

$99; ☺8am-10:30pm Sun-Wed, 8am-midnight Thu-Sat)

Graceland Wedding Chapel   CHAPEL

11 ◉ MAP P124, C4

Offering the original Elvis imper-sonator wedding (from $199) for over 50 years. If it's good enough for rock stars, then it's probably good enough for you, too. (☎702-382-0091; www.gracelandchapel.com; 619 S Las Vegas Blvd; ☺9am-11pm)

Eating

eat   CAFE $

12 🍴 MAP P124 ,C8

Community spirit and creative cooking with mostly local products provide reason enough to venture off Fremont St for this breakfast and lunchtime gem. With a con-crete floor and spare decor, it can get loud while folks treat them-selves to truffled egg sandwiches, cinnamon biscuits with strawberry compote, shrimp po'boy sand-wiches or bowls of green chile chicken posole. (☎702-534-1515; https://eatdtlv.chefnatalieyoung.com; 707 Carson Ave; mains $8-15; ☺8am-3pm Mon-Fri, to 2pm Sat & Sun; ❄; 🚌Deuce, BHX)

La Comida   MEXICAN $$

13 🍴 MAP P124, D3

La Comida serves up authentic Mexican dishes (soups, salads, tacos, enchiladas), in a welcoming environment conducive to making new friends. Throw some tequila into the mix (the restaurant has more varieties than it does seats), straight up or in sweet and salty margaritas, and get your Downtown evening started right. (☏702-463-9900; www.lacomidalv.com; 100 6th St; mains $13-22; ☺noon-10:30pm Tue-Thu, to midnight Fri & Sat, to 11pm Sun)

Andiamo Steakhouse

STEAK $$$

14 🍴 MAP P124,C3

Of all the old-school steakhouses inside Downtown's carpet joints, the current front-runner is Joe Vicari's Andiamo Steakhouse. Upstairs from the casino, richly upholstered half-moon booths and impeccably polite waiters

set the tone for a classic Italian steakhouse feast of surf-and-turf platters and housemade pasta, followed by a rolling dessert cart. Extensive Californian and European wine list. Reservations recommended. (☏702-388-2220; www.thed.com/dining/andiamo-steak-house/; 301 Fremont St E, The D; mains $26-69; ☺5-11pm; 🚌Deuce, SDX)

Drinking

Velveteen Rabbit

COCKTAIL BAR

15 🍸 MAP P124, B6

Las Vegas wasn't always a shining neon star of craft cocktailery, but in recent years next-gen lounges like Velveteen Rabbit have put the city on the mixology map. Located in the smoothly beautified Arts District, it's a lively warren of artsy

Vegas Weddings

Velveteen Rabbit (p129)

decor with imaginative cocktails, a dozen craft beers on tap and a patio for mingling al fresco. (☎702-685-9645; http://velveteenrabbitlv.com; 1218 S Main St; ☺5pm-1am Mon-Wed, to 2am Thu-Sat, 5pm-midnight Sun; ☒108)

ReBAR

BAR

16 ☒ MAP P124, B6

Las Vegas definitely revels in kitsch, and it absolutely loves drinking spots. ReBAR unites both. Located in the Arts District, it's a temple of nutty craft items, vintage bar signs, outrageous beer steins and one-of-a-kind doohickeys. Peruse the walls for that perfect retro souvenir, then sit down for a respectable selection of beers and spirits. Bask in the vintage

glow. (☎702-349-2283; www.rebarlv.com; 1225 S Main St; ☺1pm-midnight Sun-Wed, to 1am Thu, to 2am Fri & Sat; ☒Deuce)

Downtown Cocktail Room

LOUNGE

17 ☒ MAP P124, C3

With a serious list of classic cocktails and housemade potions, this low-lit drinking den is a local darling beloved by creative types and off-duty barstaff and a top spot in the Fremont East district. The entrance is ingeniously disguised: the door looks like just another part of the wall until you discover the sweet spot you have to push to get in. Happy hour runs 4pm to 7pm Monday to Saturday. (☎702-880-3696; www.downtowncocktailroom.com; 111 S Las Vegas Blvd; cocktails $12-13; ☺4pm-2am Mon-Sat; ☒Deuce)

Triple 7

MICROBREWERY

This easygoing microbrewery (see 9 ◉ Map p124, B2) inside Main Street Station's casino (p127) pours samplers of its craft beers, particularly hoppy IPAs, as well as red, amber and golden ales, smoky porter and fruity seasonal brews like blueberry wheat beer or dark cherry stout. Happy hour runs 3pm to 6pm weekdays. (☎702-387-1896; www.mainstreetcasino.com; 200 N Main St, Main Street Station; ☺11am-7am; ☒SDX)

Entertainment

Smith Center for the Performing Arts PERFORMING ARTS

18 ⭐ MAP P124, A4

Brilliant acoustics and art-deco-inspired design are just part of the wow factor at this Downtown performing arts complex. It's also sustainably built, making it the first performing arts center of its size to achieve Silver Leadership in Energy and Environmental Design (LEED) status. Cabaret jazz, Broadway shows, classical and contemporary music, dance troupes and comedians are all on offer. (📞702-749-2000; www.thesmithcenter.com; 361 Symphony Park Ave, Symphony Park; tickets from $20; 🕑schedule varies; 🚌SDX)

Shopping

Buffalo Exchange CLOTHING

19 🔒 MAP P124, B6

A cut above your normal vintage emporium, savvy secondhand clothing chain Buffalo Exchange features racks of primarily '90s & 2000s club wear, jeans, sportswear, costumes and even designer clothes. You can also trade in your nearly new garb for cash or credit to finance your new wardrobe. We dare you to walk away empty-handed. (📞702-791-3960; www.buffaloexchange.com; 1209 S Main St; 🕑10am-7pm Mon-Sat, from 11am Sun; 🚌109, 202)

Gamblers General Store GIFTS & SOUVENIRS

20 🔒 MAP P124, B5

This authentic gaming supply superstore has it all, starting with one of Nevada's largest inventories of vintage and new slot machines, as well as full-size roulette, poker, craps and blackjack tables. Less expensive gambling paraphernalia makes for perfect Sin City souvenirs, including customizable poker chips, rainbow-colored dice and collectible decks of cards actually used in Vegas casinos. (📞702-382-9903; www.gamblersgeneralstore.com; 800 S Main St; 🕑9am-5:30pm, to 4:30pm Sun; 🚌108, Deuce)

Rainbow Feather Dyeing Co GIFTS & SOUVENIRS

21 🔒 MAP P124, B5

Where to satisfy that boa fetish? Need turkey, chicken, duck, goose, pheasant, ostrich or peacock quills? Rainbow stocks a positively fabulous selection of fine feathers and fans for Vegas showgirl costumes in every possible hue, from fire-engine red and hot pink to neon green and jet black. (📞702-598-0988; www.rainbowfeatherco.com; 1036 S Main St; 🕑9am-4pm Mon-Fri, to 1pm Sat; 🚌108, Deuce)

Worth a Trip 👀
Survey the Mighty Grand Canyon

The Grand Canyon is the USA's best-known natural attraction. Measuring more than 275 miles long and over a mile deep, it's an incredible spectacle of rock strata. After initially being dismissed by Spanish colonizers and Western pioneers as little more than an obstacle to exploration, in the late 19th century the canyon drew miners bent on exploiting its natural resources. Later, tourists arrived, seeking a romanticized wilderness ideal. When President Theodore Roosevelt visited in 1903, he sagely remarked, 'You cannot improve on it.'

👁

☎ 928-638-7888

www.nps.gov/grca

20 South Entrance Rd

🕐 7-day entry per car/person $35/20

Five-hour drive from Las Vegas

Sweeping Vistas

Carved by the Colorado River, the canyon's peaks, buttes and rims give access to fantastic vistas. Descending into its depths on hiking and mule-riding trails reveals an amazing variety of landscape, wildlife and climates. For panoramic views of the canyon's geological layer cake, head over to Yavapai Observation Station.

Driving along the Canyon Rim

The canyon rim is paralleled on the south side by a 33-mile paved scenic drive. The canyon dips in and out of view as the road passes through the piñon-juniper and ponderosa pine forests. Pullouts along the way offer jaw-dropping views, and interpretive signs explain the natural history.

Hermit Road Scenic Route

Hermit Road Scenic Route follows the South Rim on the west side of Grand Canyon Village along Hermit Rd. Closed to private vehicles March to November, the road is serviced by the free park shuttle bus; cycling is encouraged because of the light traffic. Stops offer spectacular views, and signs explain canyon features.

Desert View Drive

Open to cars year round, Desert View Drive starts to the east of Grand Canyon Village and follows the canyon rim for 26 miles to Desert View, the eastern entrance to the park. Pullouts offer spectacular views, and interpretive signs explain canyon features and geology.

Desert View Watchtower

Desert View Drive offers access to the 800-year old pueblo ruins behind the Tusayan Museum of Native American history and culture – not to mention the enchanting five-story-high **Desert View Watchtower** (928-638-8960; https://www.nps.gov/places/000/desert-view-watchtower.htm; Desert View, Desert View Dr; 8am-7pm Apr-Sep, to 6pm Oct-Mar; stairs close 30min before closing; P), the highest point on the South Rim. Unparalleled views take in not only the canyon and the Colorado River, but also the San Francisco Peaks, the Navajo Reservation and the Painted Desert.

★ Top Tips

○ Open year-round, the South Rim is the most popular jumping-off point for exploring the park.

○ Free park shuttles operate along three well-traveled routes.

○ It's a 215-mile, five-hour drive between the South and North Rim visitor centers.

○ Mule rides and rafting trips require advance planning.

✕ Take a Break

Grand Canyon Village is a convenient stopping point. After browsing the native crafts and local art on display in town, have cocktails on the back porch of the majestic **El Tovar Hotel** (advanced reservations 888-297-2757, reservations within 48hr 928-638-2631; www.grandcanyon-lodges.com; Rim Trail, Grand Canyon Village Historic District; r $263-354; year-round; P ; Village west-bound (Train Depot stop)). On the North Rim, try Grand Canyon Lodge Dining Room (p135).

Rim Trail

Hiking along the South Rim is among park visitors' favorite pastimes, with options for every skill level. Beginning in Grand Canyon Village, the **Rim Trail** (www.nps.gov/grca; Hermits Rest to South Kaibab Trailhead; 👣; 🚌 Village, 🚌 Kaibab/Rim, 🚌 Hermits Rest (Mar 1-Nov 30)) is the most popular, and easiest. It dips into the pines of Kaibab National Forest and connects a series of scenic points and historical sights over 13 miles.

Bright Angel Trail

The most popular of the corridor trails is beautiful **Bright Angel Trail** (www.nps.gov/grca; Rim Trail, Grand Canyon Village Historic District; 👣; 🚌 Village, 🚌 Hermits Rest (Mar 1-Nov 30)). The steep and scenic 7.8-mile descent to the Colorado River is punctuated with four logical turnaround spots. Summer heat can be crippling; day hikers should either turn around at one of the resthouses (a 3- to 6-mile round trip) or hit the trail at dawn.

South Kaibab Trail

The South Kaibab (South Rim) is one of the park's prettiest trails, combining stunning scenery and unobstructed, 360-degree views. Steep, rough and wholly exposed, summer ascents can be dangerous, and during this season rangers discourage all but the shortest day hikes – otherwise it's a six-mile, grueling round trip. Turning around after 1.5 miles at Cedar Ridge makes for a fine short day hike.

Horseback Riding in the Canyon

Due to erosion concerns, the National Park Service (NPS) no longer allows one-day mule rides down into the canyon. **Canyon Vistas Mule Rides** (📞 888-297-2757, next-day reservations 928-638-2631; www.grandcanyonlodges.com/plan/mule-rides; Bright Angel Lodge, Grand Canyon Village Historic District; 2hr mule ride $143, 1-/2-night mule ride incl meals & accommodations $606/875; per 2 people $1057/1440; ⏱ rides available year-round, hours vary; 👣) offers a three-hour trip along a newly constructed four-mile trail beside the east rim or a two-day trip to the bottom of the canyon, which includes a night at Phantom Ranch.

Flying over the Canyon

Helicopter and airplane flights over the canyon have been restricted in number, altitude and routes to reduce noise pollution affecting other visitors and wildlife. Companies offering scenic flyovers include **Grand Canyon Airlines** (📞 702-638-3300; www.grandcanyonairlines.com; 871 Liberator Dr, Grand Canyon Village, AZ 86023; from $159) and **Papillon Grand Canyon Helicopters** (📞 702-736-7243, 888-635-7272; www.papillon.com; 1265 Airport Rd, Boulder City, NV 89005; 45min from $124). Contact them for specific rates, as each offers several options. Most flights leave from Tusayan and Las Vegas, but check itinerary and departure points carefully; Grand Canyon West is not part of Grand Canyon National Park.

Geology of the Grand Canyon

The Grand Canyon captivates travelers because of its sheer immensity: it's a tableau that reveals the earth's history layer by dramatic layer. Mother Nature adds artistic details – rugged plateaus, crumbly spires, shadowed ridges – that flirt and catch your eye as the sun crosses the sky.

A River Runs Through It

Snaking along the canyon floor are 277 miles of the Colorado River, which has carved out the canyon over the past six million years and has exposed rocks up to two billion years old – half the age of the earth. The sequences of rocks include layers of limestone, sandstone, shale, granite and schist. At the Yavapai Observation Station on the South Rim, visitors can walk an interpretive trail that explains how these layers were formed over time.

History Written on the Walls

Stand in the basin and look up: the Grand Canyon's towering walls are a mile high, offering a fascinating cross section of the earth's crust. Forget millions of years – these walls represent two billion years of the earth's history. A guide can point out the crystalline rocks, likely the product of long-ago lava flows, in the trio of 'Granite Gorges.' Geologists estimate that these rocks metamorphosed around 1.75 billion years ago.

North Rim, South Rim

The two rims of the Grand Canyon offer quite different experiences; they lie more than 200 miles apart by road and are rarely visited on the same trip. Most visitors choose the South Rim for its easy access, wealth of services and vistas that don't disappoint. The quieter North Rim has its own charms: at 8200ft elevation (1000ft higher than the South Rim), its cooler temperatures support verdant meadows and tall, thick groves of trees. Head here for solitude in nature's bounty – only 10% of park visitors make the trek. Meadows are thick with wildflowers and dense clusters of willowy aspen and spruce trees, the air is often crisp and the skies big and blue.

Grand Canyon Lodge Dining Room

The windows are so huge at **Grand Canyon Lodge Dining Room** (☑May-Oct 928-638-8560; www.grandcanyonforever.com/dining; breakfast $8-11, lunch $10-15, dinner $18-35; ⏰6:30-10am, 11:30am-2:30pm & 4:30-9:30pm May 15-Oct 15; 🖉🚼) that you can sit anywhere and enjoy good views over the North Rim. The menu includes regional treats such as western trout and buffalo flank steak. Reservations essential.

El Tovar Dining Room & Lounge

A stone's throw from the canyon's edge, **El Tovar** (☑928-638-2631; www.grandcanyonlodges.com/dine/el-tovar-dining-room-and-lounge; El Tovar, Grand Canyon Village Historic District; mains $20-30; ⏰restaurant 6:30-10:30am, 11:15am-2pm & 4:30-9:30pm, lounge 11:30am-11pm; 🅿🚼;

Village) has the best views of any restaurant in the state, if not the country. The grand stone-and-dark-oak dining room warms the soul like an upscale lodge of yore. Reservations are required for dinner. To avoid the lunchtime crowds, arrive before 11:45am.

River Rafting

Rafting the Colorado ranks among the top outdoor adventures of a lifetime – not just for the thrill (the water is BIG), but also for the epic scenery and exploration. It's a placid geological journey through time, an adrenaline rush, a jagged desert landscape and lush riparian paradise all rolled into one phenomenal ride.

Most experience the river on a commercial rafting trip between mid-April and September (for motorized boats) or November (for oared vessels). Though the park carefully regulates the number of rafts on the Colorado, during this high season you won't be alone, often sharing hikes and beaches with visitors on other trips.

For those on tight schedules, commercial motorized tours can show you half the canyon in four days, or the full thing in seven. This is a bit like watching your favorite movie on fast-forward: you'll get the general idea, but miss everything that makes it great. The longer you can spend, the better.

A few hundred private rafting excursions are allowed on the river as well; they launch year-round after securing permits via a lottery. Some people wait decades for the right opportunity.

Grand Canyon National Park

While there are no day trips through Grand Canyon National Park itself, there are two options outside the park. The Hualapai Reservation offers a white-water day trip that includes bus pickup in Williams, a drive to the canyon bottom, and a helicopter ride back out of the canyon. Several tour operators offer half-day smooth-water trips between Glen Canyon Dam and Lee's Ferry.

Rock Climbing

Rock climbing is allowed anywhere in the Grand Canyon – except above established trails (for obvious reasons) – but while Arizona is rife with climbing areas, scaling the canyon is not popular. That being said, almost any boulder or wall is begging to be scaled, just beware of loose, dirty and chalky rock.

Most climbers tend to target the canyon's remote temples (spires carved by converging side canyons) which can involve multiday approaches and creative route-finding. Mountaineers who plan to hike in and camp will need a backcountry permit. Bolting is not allowed inside the park.

Stop by **Flagstaff Climbing** (📞928-556-9909; www.flagstaffclimbing.com; day pass $16; ⏰10am-10pm Mon-Fri, noon-8pm Sat & Sun) in Flagstaff for information on climbing throughout the region. Stewart M Green's Rock Climbing Arizona (Falcon, 1999) is a comprehensive guide to prime Arizona crags and includes topographical maps and detailed route information.

Grand Canyon Accommodations

Accommodations in the park range from historic lodges to rustic cabins to standard motel rooms (book 13 months in advance). There are developed campgrounds as well as backcountry campsites, where you can roll out your sleeping bag under the stars to experience an unforgettable sunrise. Casting a wider net opens up any number of accommodation options in nearby towns.

In the South Rim region, Williams, Sedona and Flagstaff have several B&Bs. Hosts tend to be knowledgeable about the area and offer great advice on things to see and do in their hometowns and at the canyon. Most don't welcome children.

Inside the park, lodges are basically the park's hotels, where the rooms are comfortable enough but very basic. The exceptions are the South Rim's **El Tovar** (📞888-297-2757, 928-638-2631; www.grandcanyonlodges.com; $263-354; P🛜❄️👪) and **Bright Angel Lodge cabins** (📞888-297-2757, 928-638-2631; www.grandcanyonlodges.com; dm $65, cabin d $169, available by lottery; P🛜👪). **Phantom Ranch** (📞888-297-2757, 928-638-2631; www.grandcanyonlodges.com; $263-354; ❄️👪) on the canyon bottom is a basic summer-camp affair, but feels like paradise after a long day of dusty hiking.

In Sedona and Las Vegas, full-service resorts offer luxury accommodations, beautiful surrounds, excellent restaurants and first-class service. Many offer on-site spas, activities and elegant pools.

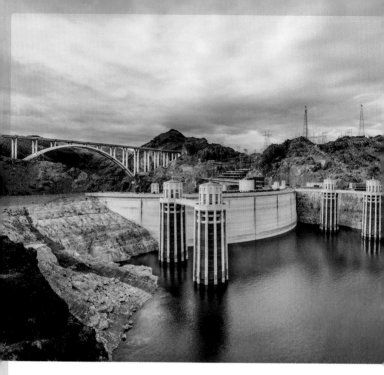

Worth a Trip 🔭
Marvel at Hoover Dam & Lake Mead

Even those who question the USA's commitment to damming the US West have to marvel at the engineering and architecture of the Hoover Dam. Set amid the almost unbearably dry Mojave Desert, the dam towers over Black Canyon, the stretch of the Colorado River just below Hoover Dam, providing electricity for the entire region. Hoover Dam created Lake Mead, which boasts 700 miles of shoreline, while Davis Dam created the much smaller Lake Mohave, which straddles the Arizona border.

◉

📞 866-730-9097, 702-494-2517

www.usbr.gov/lc/hoo verdam

off Hwy 93

incl parking $10

🕘 9am-5pm

👫

Hoover Dam Tour

Guided tours of the architectural wonder begin at the visitor center. Take an elevator ride 50 stories below to view the dam's massive power generators, each of which alone could power a city of 100,000 people.

Boulder City/Hoover Dam Museum

You'll enjoy the dam tour more if you stop at the small but engagingly hands-on Hoover Dam Museum first. Exhibits focus on Depression-era America and the tough living conditions endured by the people who built the dam. A 20-minute film features historical footage of the project.

Mike O'Callaghan-Pat Tillman Memorial Bridge

Featuring a pedestrian walkway with perfect views upstream of Hoover Dam, the **Mike O'Callaghan-Pat Tillman Memorial Bridge** (Hwy 93) was named for Mike O'Callaghan, governor of Nevada from 1971 to 1979, and NFL star turned US Army Ranger Pat Tillman. Tillman, once a player for the Arizona Cardinals, was killed by friendly fire in Afghanistan in 2004.

Lake Mead National Recreational Area

It's less than an hour's drive from Las Vegas to the most visited northern section of the 1.5-million-acre **Lake Mead National Recreation Area** (info desk 702-293-8906, visitor center 702-293-8990; www.nps.gov/lake; Lakeshore Scenic Dr; 7-day entry per vehicle $25; 24hr;), a popular weekend camping destination for local residents. Within this protected area of the Mojave Desert are Lake Mead, which extends 110 miles toward the Grand Canyon; 67-mile-long Lake Mohave, which runs along the Arizona–Nevada border; and miles of spectacular desert around the lakes.

★ **Getting There**

Hoover Dam is located 30 miles southeast of Las Vegas.

○ It's a 40-minute drive from the Strip.

○ Take a day-long guided tour from the city.

★ **Top Tips**

○ At Hoover Dam, park for free on the other side of the Arizona state line and walk to the visitor center.

○ Several companies on the Strip offer guided bus tours to Hoover Dam.

✕ **Take a Break**

Stop in Boulder City at a classic diner like the **Coffee Cup** (p141), or go for sandwiches and wine at lively **Milo's Cellar** (p141).

Water Sports on Lake Mead

Popular year-round activities on the lake include swimming, fishing, boating, paddleboarding, water skiing and kayaking; **Vegas Watersports** (📞702-748-7873; https://lakelasvegaswatersports.com; 490 Horsepower Cove; 🕑6am-10pm) offers return transport from your hotel. A splendid scenic drive winds north along Lakeshore Dr and Northshore Rd, passing viewpoints, hiking and birding trailheads, beaches and bays, and full-service marinas.

Hiking from Lake to Dam

A 3.7-mile hiking trail along a historical railway line with five tunnels links Lake Mead's **Alan Bible Visitor Center** (Alan Bible Visitor Center; 📞702-293-8990; www.nps.gov/lake; Lakeshore Scenic Dr, off US Hwy 93; per vehicle $25; 🕑9am-4:30pm) to Hoover Dam. The most challenging hike in the park follows a 3-mile trail down 800ft to a set of hot springs in a slot off Black Canyon.

A Leisurely Lunchtime Cruise

Lake Mead Cruises (📞702-293-6180; www.lakemeadcruises.com; Lakeshore Rd; 90min cruise adult/child from $28/14; 👶) offers kid-friendly tours, along with lunch and brunch cruises, on a triple-decker, air conditioned, Mississippi-style paddle wheeler. It departs from Hemenway Harbor.

Guided Adventures in the Desert

Let the outdoor experts show you the stunning landscape up close and personal. **Desert Adventures** (📞702-293-5026; www.kayaklasvegas.com; 1647 Nevada Hwy; full-day Colorado River kayak $195; 🕑9am-6pm Apr-Oct, 10am-4pm Nov-Mar) runs a range of half-, full- and multiday kayaking adventures on the Colorado River, as well as fishing, hiking and boating guided tours – including smooth water floats on the Colorado River through Black Canyon ($169). It also arranges multiday tours of the Grand Canyon, Zion and Bryce, and other outdoor tours.

Boulder City

On your way back to Las Vegas, stop for a stroll and a bite to eat in the relaxed but charming town of Boulder City, a rare casino-free town in Nevada. The town was originally erected to house workers constructing the Hoover Dam; today, it's a pleasant stop for travelers. Breakfast is served all day at

Paddleboarding on Lake Mead

History of Hoover Dam

A statue of bronze winged figures stands atop Hoover Dam, memorializing those who built the massive 726ft concrete structure – one of the world's tallest dams. The ambitious project resulted in a high number of human casualties, a fact many tourists don't realize as they're snapping pictures.

First Dam on the Colorado

Originally called Boulder Dam and later renamed after President Herbert Hoover, the Colorado River's first major dam was conceived as a New Deal public works project. Construction began in 1931, at the height of the Depression. Thousands of unemployed men – upwards of 10,000 and as many as 20,000 – arrived in Black Canyon with their families, eager for work.

Tough Working Conditions

The settlement of Boulder City was planned to house workers, but accommodations weren't ready for the first wave; migrant families had to arrange their own housing. Conditions at the work site were bleak – desert temperatures soared to 120°F (49°C) and there were few available services in the area. The dam was the largest concrete structure of its kind ever to be built, and building efforts were characterized by risk, with some workers dangling hundreds of feet above the canyon. Sadly, hundreds lost their lives. But construction kept moving forward, the dam going up ahead of schedule and the new town of Boulder City growing. Casinos were outlawed there to prevent workers becoming distracted from their daytime task.

Glory Days

Hoover Dam was completed early, and under budget, in 1936. President Franklin D Roosevelt was present for the official dedication; afterwards, FDR continued on to Las Vegas – the first time a US president had paid a visit to Sin City. Several other famous figures – including Bette Davis and Howard Hughes – spent the night at the historic Boulder Dam Hotel after the dam was finished. Today, the historic hotel is the home of the Hoover Dam Museum. Confirming the dam's significance as a symbol of national pride, the landmark was closed to the public for the duration of WWII, and again in 1963 and 1969 after the respective deaths of Presidents Kennedy and Eisenhower.

the **Coffee Cup** (☏702-294-0517; www.worldfamouscoffeecup.com; 512 Nevada Way; mains $6-10; ⊙6am-2pm; 👶), a downtown diner with a gourmet spin, while cozy **Milo's**

Cellar (☏702-293-9540; www.milosbouldercity.com; 534 Nevada Hwy; mains $9-14; ⊙11am-9pm) serves wine and cheese in the evening.

Survival Guide

Las Vegas Monorail S-F/SHUTTERSTOCK ©

Before You Go

Book Your Stay

Useful Websites

Lonely Planet (www. lonelyplanet.com/ hotels) Book hotels and other accommodations.

Vegas.com (www. vegas.com) Local online travel agent exclusively servicing Las Vegas.

Travelzoo (www.travel zoo.com) For discount hotel deals.

Priceline (www.price line.com) Lets you bid or 'express' buy your hotel room for less.

Travelworm (www. travelworm.com) Comprehensive hotel listings and promos.

Best Budget

Downtown Grand (www.downtowngrand. com) Good-value digs in the heart of Downtown.

Golden Nugget (www. goldennugget.com)

When to Go

○ **Spring (Mar–May)** Perfect weather and steady crowds; the conference set will be reserving blocks of hotel rooms.

○ **Summer (Jun–Aug)** Dog days of summer. Too hot to enjoy outdoor activities, except at night.

○ **Fall (Sep & Oct)** Balmy temperatures make Vegas a pleasant getaway. Hotel room competition heats up with plenty of conferences in town.

○ **Winter (Nov–Feb)** The chilliest time of year; the famous pool bars shut down during these months.

This local legend wins top points for Downtown's best rooms and amenities.

El Cortez (www. elcortezhotelcasino. com) For something a little different, where old meets new Downtown.

Thunderbird Hotel (www.thunderbird hotellasvegas.com) Funky, fresh rooms with reclaimed-wood furniture and a fun, youthful vibe.

Best Midrange

LINQ Hotel (www. caesars.com/linq) You can't beat LINQ for value and its center-Strip location.

SLS (www.slslas vegas.com) A north Strip location means incredible rates for this boutique brand.

Platinum Hotel & Spa (www.theplatinum hotel.com) This non-gaming, nonsmoking hotel near the Strip has sanctuary-like suites.

Money-Saving Tips

o If you're trying to lock in a good rate at a popular resort, call the hotel directly and ask about special promotions or better rates on unremodeled rooms.

o Don't make room reservations on the weekend; rates often drop across the board on Monday mornings.

o For live entertainment, save cash by scoring last-minute tickets at **Tix4Tonight** (www. tix4tonight.com).

o Take advantage of such free attractions as the Fountains at Bellagio, the Burlesque Hall of Fame, the Mirage Volcano, the Fremont Street Experience and the outdoor Neon Museum.

o Get free drinks while playing the slots (but do tip).

Aria Las Vegas Resort (www.arialasvegas.com) Sleek resort hotel where every room has a corner view.

Sahara Las Vegas (www.saharalasvegas.com) If you like design and a cooler crowd, hang at this 2019 newcomer.

Best Top End

Encore (www.wynnlasvegas.com) Excellence at every turn.

Signature at MGM Grand (www.signa

turemgmgrand.com) Indulgent suites atop the massive megalopolis of MGM Grand.

Four Seasons Hotel (www.fourseasons. com/lasvegas) , Mandalay Bay's luxury offering doesn't fail to impress.

Mandarin Oriental (www.mandarinoriental.com) Luscious oriental flavors meet the latest technology.

Cosmopolitan (www. cosmopolitanlasvegas.com) Hippest Strip rooms with

sunken tubs, balconies and design quirks.

Arriving in Las Vegas

McCarran International Airport

o The easiest and cheapest way to get to your hotel is by airport shuttle (one-way to Strip/downtown hotels from $7/9) or a shared ride-share service like Uber or Lyft (from $10). As you exit baggage claim, look for shuttle bus kiosks lining the curb; prices and destinations are clearly marked.

o Taxis hover at $15 to $25 for the Strip and upwards of $20 for Downtown, plus tip.

o If you're renting a car from the airport, catch a shuttle bus outside baggage claim to the McCarran Rent-a-Car Center.

Be Forewarned

o **Smoking** If cigarette smoke bothers you, steer clear of older casinos and gamble at the airier Wynn/Encore, Venetian/Palazzo or Bellagio.

o **Sex workers** Prostitution is illegal in Clark County, but escorts, call girls and working girls are part of Sin City's high-rolling culture.

o **Resort fees** Think you scored a deal on your hotel room? Most hotels add mandatory daily 'resort fees' of $10 to $30, which may cover internet access and fitness-center entry, or nothing much at all. Some also charge $10 for phone reservations.

Driving into Las Vegas

o The main roads into and out of Las Vegas are the I-15 Fwy and US Hwy 95. US Hwy 93 connects Downtown with Hoover Dam. I-215 goes by McCarran International Airport.

o When traffic is snarled on I-15 and Las Vegas Blvd, stick to surface routes, such as Paradise Rd, east of the Strip; or Frank Sinatra Dr and Industrial Rd, west of the Strip.

o The fastest way to get across the Strip and I-15 is via the Desert Inn Rd super-arterial.

Getting Around

Bus

o **RTC** (Regional Transportation Commission of Southern Nevada; ☎702-228-7433; www.rtcsnv.com/transit; 2/24/72hr bus pass $6/8/20, child under 5yr free) buses operate from 5am to 2am daily, with popular Strip and Downtown routes running 24/7 every 15 to 20 minutes. RTC's double-decker Deuce buses to/from Downtown stop every block or two along the Strip; quicker SDX

(Strip & Downtown Express) buses stop outside some Strip casino hotels, as well as at the Fashion Show, the city's convention center and a few off-Strip shopping malls.

o Many off-Strip casino hotels offer limited shuttle buses to/from the Strip, usually reserved for hotel guests.

Car & Motorcycle

o Driving on the Strip can be stressful. As of April 2017, self-parking at Strip casinos is no longer free.

o International short-term visitors only need their home license to rent or drive a car or motorcycle. If your license isn't written in English, you may be required to show an international driving permit (IDP).

Monorail

o The **Las Vegas Monorail** (☎702-699-8299; www.lvmonorail.com; single ride $5, 24/72hr pass $13/29; ☺7am-midnight Mon, to 2am Tue-Thu, to 3am Fri-Sun) links some Strip casino resorts, zipping between MGM Grand,

What to Bring

Classy clothes Women can get away with jeans, but a dress code is loosely enforced at the best nightclubs and restaurants.

Comfortable shoes If you want to explore the Strip, you'll need something supportive.

Camera Be prepared to snap.

Bally's/Paris, Flamingo/Caesars, Harrah's/LINQ, Las Vegas Convention Center, Westgate and Sahara.

o Although service is frequent (every four to 12 minutes), stations are only on the east side of the Strip, set back from Las Vegas Blvd at the rear of the casinos.

o Trains are air-conditioned and stroller- and wheelchair-friendly.

Shuttle

o Many off-Strip casino hotels offer limited free shuttle buses to and from the Strip, although some are reserved for hotel guests.

o Free public shuttles connect the Rio with Harrah's and Bally's/Paris Las Vegas usually every 30 minutes from 10am until 1am daily.

Taxi & Limousine

o It's illegal to hail a cab on the street. Instead, taxi stands are found at almost every casino hotel and shopping mall.

Walking the Strip

The Strip runs for miles: don't assume you can easily walk from point A to B. Consult a map first and note that pedestrian crossings are punctuated with sky bridges and escalators. Take advantage of free trams between casinos whenever possible.

o Vegas is surprisingly compact, so taxis can be reasonable on a per-trip basis. A lift from one end of the Strip to the other, or from mid-Strip to Downtown, costs at least $20, depending on traffic.

o Tip the driver 10% to 15%, rounded up to the nearest dollar.

o For special occasions or stepping out in style, some parties will hire a limousine. Presidential Limo is a popular company.

o A good resource is www.vegas.com/transportation/las-vegas-taxis.

Tram

Free public air-conditioned trams shuttle all day long between some Strip casino hotels. One connects the Bellagio, CityCenter and the Monte Carlo. Another links Treasure Island and the Mirage. A third zips between Excalibur, Luxor and Mandalay Bay.

Renting a Car

Booking online through a car-rental agency or a discount travel website normally nets you the best rates. Economy car-rental rates start at $25/145 per day/week, though you might find a much cheaper deal by looking online ahead of time. Expect to pay extra for insurance (usually optional), taxes of over 10% and government surcharges of 10%. A facility charge (almost $4 per day) and 10% airport fee often apply as well. Most companies require a major credit card, and some require that the driver be at least 25 years old.

Essential Information

Accessible Travel

o Vegas has the most ADA-accessible guestrooms in the USA. Almost all attractions are wheelchair-accessible.

o Wheelchair seating is widely available and assisted listening devices are offered at most showrooms.

o Most public transportation and several hotel pools are elevator-equipped.

o By law, all taxi companies must have a wheelchair-accessible van.

Business Hours

Bars 5pm–3am as a general rule

Casinos 24 hours year-round

Restaurants hours vary wildly, but generally 11am–2pm for lunch and 5pm–10pm for dinner

Shops 10am–9pm (to 6pm Sunday), closed Christmas Day; to 11pm in casinos

Discounts

o Check **Smarter Vegas** (www.smartervegas.com) for promotional discount codes for sights, tours, shows and hotels.

o A multiday **Las Vegas Power Pass** (www.lasvegaspowerpass.com) may be worthwhile if you plan to visit a lot of big-ticket attractions and museums; it even lets you skip the lines at some of them.

Tips on Tipping

Keep small bills on hand. Leave a poor tip for remarkably lousy service, or in exceptionally bad (rare) cases, none at all. Reward exceptional service. Minimum tipping standards:

o **Hotels** Porters: $1 to $2 per bag; housekeeping $1 to $2 per night; valet $2 to $5 (paid when keys returned)

o **Restaurants** 15% to 25% of total bill

o **Bars/casinos** $1 per drink or 15% per round

o **Taxis/limos** 15% of fare, at your discretion

Electricity

Type A
120V/60Hz

Type B
120V/60Hz

Emergencies

o **Police, fire, ambulance** (911)

LGBTIQ+ Travelers

Let's be clear: it's perfectly OK to be 'out' in Vegas. It's a place where you can be who you are and even be who you wanna be, but as with most places, don't be surprised if wildly flamboyant behavior is met with rudeness or disdain. Americans are generally friendly, respectful people. Respect the rules and behaviors of those around you, and you'll inevitably be treated in the same way.

Money

o All casinos, banks and shopping malls, and most convenience stores, have ATMs.

o Cold hard cash greases Sin City's wheels. You'll want to have bills of various sizes on hand, partly so you're ready to tip when necessary.

o Casinos charge ridiculous rates for currency exchange.

o Credit cards are widely accepted. All casinos will advance cash against plastic but fees are exorbitant.

Public Holidays

Note that the only holiday that shops always close for is Christmas.

The Lowdown on Smoking

'Smoke-free' and 'Las Vegas' are rarely mentioned in the same sentence: there are ashtrays at almost every telephone, elevator and swimming pool – even in toilets and taxis. A limited ban on smoking inside public buildings, including restaurants, shops and movie theaters, went into effect in 2006, but exceptions still permit smoking inside casinos, as well as at bars and clubs that don't serve prepared food. Most casino hotels claim to offer nonsmoking rooms, but don't expect the air to be free of a whiff of cigarettes.

New Year's Day January 1

Martin Luther King Jr Day Third Monday in January

Presidents' Day Third Monday in February

Good Friday Friday before Easter in March/April

Memorial Day Last Monday in May

Independence Day July 4

Labor Day First Monday in September

Columbus Day Second Monday in October

Veterans Day November 11

Thanksgiving Day Fourth Thursday in November

Christmas Day December 25

Responsible Travel

o Tear yourself away from the Strip to explore offbeat museums, historic sites, spectacular scenery and characterful drinking and dining options.

o Frequent local cafes and restaurants using organic and regional ingredients and offering plant-based options. Choose wisely at all-you-can-eat buffets.

o Stay at LEED-certified properties (eg Aria, Vdara), solar-powered ones (eg Mandalay Bay, Wynn) and others focused on footprint-friendly technologies and practices.

o Travel to Las Vegas by coach – Flixbus (flixbus.com) operates direct routes from LA, San Francisco and other southwestern cities.

o Get around by public bus or such free transport options as the Monorail, trams, shuttle buses and your own two feet.

o If you rent a car, make it a hybrid or electric vehicle.

Safe Travel

o The US reopened to vaccinated air travelers from dozens of countries, including China, Brazil and most of Europe, in September 2021. Contact the US embassy in your country or check the State Department's website (http://travel.state.gov) for the latest entry rules.

o Find current Las Vegas–specific COVID-19 requirements and mitigation measures at https://nvhealth response.nv.gov.

o On the Strip and the Fremont Street Experience, police and private security officers are out in force, and surveillance cameras ('eyes in the sky') are omnipresent.

o Use in-room hotel safes and never leave valuables unattended, especially while gambling.

o Beware of pickpockets in crowds (eg on public transportation).

o If you wander Downtown away from Fremont St, keep your wits about you, day and night. Likewise, the area between Downtown and the Stratosphere can be sketchy.

Tourist Information

○ **Las Vegas Convention & Visitors Authority** (LVCVA; ☏877-847-4858, 702-892-7575; www.visitlasvegas.com; 3150 Paradise Rd; ⊙8am-5pm Mon-Fri; 🛜; 🚇Las Vegas Convention Center) The hotline provides up-to-date information about shows, attractions, activities and more; staff may help with finding last-minute accommodations.

○ Check out www.vegas.com for additional tourist resources and bookings.

Visas

The following information is highly subject to change. Double-check visa and passport requirements at http://travel.state.gov or with a US consulate in your country before coming to the USA.

○ Visas aren't required for citizens of the 40 Visa Waiver Program (VWP) countries, who may enter the USA for up to 90 days visa-free. Only British citizens with the unrestricted right of permanent residence in the UK qualify for the VWP.

○ However, citizens of VWP countries must still apply for travel authorization online (see https://esta.cbp.dhs.gov) at least 72 hours before traveling; registration is usually valid for two years. VWP travelers must also be in possession of a round-trip or onward ticket to enter the US. Passports must meet current US standards.

○ Temporary visitors from Canada do not normally need a visa for stays of up to 181 days, but they must bring their Canadian passport.

○ All other foreign citizens must wrangle a nonimmigrant visa in advance from a US embassy or consulate. Best done in your home country, the process costs a nonrefundable fee (minimum $160), involves a personal interview and can take several weeks, so apply early.

Behind the Scenes

Send Us Your Feedback

We love to hear from travelers – your comments help make our books better. We read every word, and we guarantee that your feedback goes straight to the authors. Visit **lonelyplanet.com/contact** to submit your updates and suggestions.

Note: We may edit, reproduce and incorporate your comments in Lonely Planet products such as guidebooks, websites and digital products, so let us know if you don't want your comments reproduced or your name acknowledged. For a copy of our privacy policy visit lonelyplanet.com/privacy.

Benedict's Thanks

A huge thank you to Alex Howard from LP for granting me this amazing opportunity and sticking by me until I got 'er done. I dedicate this update to Mr & Mrs Bruce & Cheryl Cowie, my self-adopted Canadian parents and the original high rollers of my world. Thanks to Mum for giving Nanna's prayer-chair a workout; to Kirk, Alex and friends for showing me their Vegas; to Justin and the burners in Reno, Nicole in Carson City, and my favorite American, Brad. You all rock.

Acknowledgements

Cover photograph: Paris Las Vegas reflected in CityCenter, Jon Hicks/Getty Images © Back cover photograph: Neon cowboy sign on Fremont St, Grant Faint/Getty Images ©

Photographs pp 32–3 Kit Leong/Shutterstock ©, Kris Davidson/Lonely Planet ©, Fotos593/Getty Images ©, Kit Leong/Shutterstock ©

This Book

This 6th edition of Lonely Planet's *Pocket Las Vegas* guidebook was curated by Andrea Schulte-Peevers and researched and written by Benedict Walker, who also both curated and wrote the last edition. This guidebook was produced by the following:

Destination Editor
Alexander Howard

Senior Product Editor
Sasha Drew

Product Editor
Alison Killilea

Senior Cartographer
Julie Sheridan

Book Designer
Gwen Cotter

Assisting Editors Michelle Bennett, Anne Mulvaney

Cover Researcher
Marika Mercer

Thanks to
Ronan Abayawickrema, Shona Gray, Clare Healy, Sonia Kapoor, Mani Ramaswamy, Kathryn Rowan, Saralinda Turner

Index

See also separate subindexes for:

🔘 **Eating p155**

🔘 **Drinking p156**

⭐ **Entertainment p156**

🔒 **Shopping p156**

Sights 000
Map Pages **000**

Sights **000**
Map Pages **000**

Our Writers

Andrea Schulte-Peevers

Born and raised in Germany and educated in London and at UCLA, Andrea has travelled the distance to the moon and back in her visits to some 75 countries. She has earned her living as a professional travel writer for over two decades and authored or contributed to nearly 100 Lonely Planet titles as well as to newspapers, magazines and websites. She also works as a travel consultant, translator and editor. Andrea specialises in Germany, Dubai and the UAE, Crete and the Caribbean Islands. She lives in Berlin.

Benedict Walker

Ben was born in Newcastle (NSW, Australia) and grew up in the 'burbs, spending weekends and long summers by the beach. Although he's drawn magnetically to the kinds of mountains he encountered in the Canadian Rockies and the Japanese and Swiss Alps, beach life is in his blood. A fluent Japanese speaker, his first book for LP was Japan, and he has since written on Australia, Canada, Germany, Vietnam and the USA. Find him on Instagram @wordsandjourneys.

Published by Lonely Planet Global Limited
CRN 554153
6th edition – Jul 2022
ISBN 978 1 787017399
© Lonely Planet 2022 Photographs © as indicated 2022
10 9 8 7 6 5 4 3 2 1
Printed in Singapore